Judaic Christianity

The One True Religion

THE *ONLY* WAY TO ETERNAL LIFE

STEVEN DEMERS

Tate Publishing, LLC

"Judaic Christianity" by Steven Demers

Copyright © 2005 by Steven Demers. All rights reserved.

Published in the United States of America
by Tate Publishing, LLC
127 East Trade Center Terrace
Mustang, OK 73064
(888) 361–9473

Book design copyright © 2005 by Tate Publishing, LLC. All rights reserved.

No part of this publication may be reproduced, stored in a retrieval system or transmitted in any way by any means, electronic, mechanical, photocopy, recording or otherwise without the prior permission of the author except as provided by USA copyright law.

All scripture quotations are taken from the Holy Bible, New International Version ®, Copyright © 1973, 1978, 1984 by International Bible Society. Used by permission of Zondervan Publishing House. All rights reserved.

ISBN: 1-5988600-4-6

Table of Contents

Preface 5

Introduction 7

1. RELIGION: How Many True Religions Can There Be? ... 15
2. Man's Problem - God's Solution 29
3. The Covenant of GRACE 45
4. The Long Road Back 61
5. How Bad Is the Human Race? 77
6. HOPE – the Gift of a Loving God 93
7. A World Without Light 109
8. God DID Provide! 123
9. The Cross and the Gospel 141
10. The Beginning of the Church 155
11. Jews and Gentiles: Two Peoples, One Faith 171
12. Has the Church Replaced Israel? 185

Preface

> "I am not ashamed of the gospel, because it is the power of God for the salvation of everyone who believes: first for the Jew, then for the Gentile. For in the gospel a righteousness from God is revealed, a righteousness that is by faith from first to last, just as it is written: 'The righteous will live by faith.'" - Romans 1:16–17

Sharing the conviction of the Apostle Paul, whom the Holy Spirit of God used to pen half the letters of the New Testament, I have felt compelled to write what follows in order to encourage those who may read these words to study the Bible, the Word of the one, true God. Many today have rejected the truth revealed in the Bible without ever reading and studying it for themselves. Millions are like sheep, marching to their own destruction because they follow the voices of those who speak lies. God's Word is truth! And in its pages are words of life!!

As we have entered into the twenty-first century much of our culture has determined that there is no such truth. There exists a spirit of toleration for any teaching, caused by a failure to understand that the inevitable result is confusion. Even many within the Church today refuse to proclaim Jesus Christ as the Way, the Truth and the Life. Without clear direction, the Church marches on, offering one possible alternative among a growing crowd of possibilities. The Gospel, the truth about Jesus Christ and what He came to accomplish and what yet lies ahead, has gotten lost in the midst of mankind's quest for understanding and wisdom. The truth which can be received and understood by children has been distorted and abandoned by those who claim to be wise.

The Bible is one book, one story, beginning in the mind of God before the creation of the world, and extending to eternity when Jesus returns and God rules in a new heavens and a new earth. Christianity did not begin with the birth of Jesus, the Christ, but rather is the fulfillment of biblical Judaism. Thus, the history and truth concerning God and His relationship with the nation of Israel, found in the Old Testament, forms the foundation for understanding all that begins in the life and ministry of Jesus, including His death, resurrection and ascension into heaven AND His return to earth to reign over all of creation. It is impossible to understand God's plan, His work in the world today through the Church, or what He tells us lies ahead without reading and understanding what came before.

"Judaic Christianity–the ONE True Religion" is written to all those who are seeking truth. God has revealed truth as His Spirit led the writers of Scripture, and through their words God reveals Himself to those who are given ears to hear and eyes to see and minds to understand. The Spirit of God is our Teacher and He uses the word which He caused to be written to instruct those who would know the God of truth today.

This is the "day of salvation," the "acceptable year of the LORD," the time between the birth of Jesus—the Messiah, the Christ—and His return, when God offers forgiveness and life to all who will receive Jesus, His Son, as their Savior and LORD. God's truth is available for all; the time is now! May the Spirit of God use these pages to speak to those who are searching and may they find in the Bible the truth that will set them free!!

Introduction

Do you want to live forever? That may sound like a foolish question to ask; after all, if given the opportunity, who wouldn't want to live forever? Many may even think it to be an absurd question, for no one has ownership to the formula for eternal life. Certainly, no one can speak with authority and declare that they KNOW how you and I can be SURE that we will, in fact, live forever! Who would be so foolish as to attempt to say such a thing?

Jesus would! Jesus—a man who lived upon this earth nearly two thousand years ago; a man who claimed to be much more than that, who claimed to be God, come to earth in human form in order to "save" those who would believe in Him from the judgment of God which would someday come upon all the earth. Shortly before He raised His friend, Lazarus, from the dead (Lazarus had been dead for four days), Jesus said to Lazarus' sister, Martha, "I am the resurrection and the life. He who believes in me will live, even though he dies; and whoever lives and believes in me will never die" (John 11:25–26).

Yes, Jesus boldly proclaimed that He had the power and the authority to give eternal life to all who believed in Him; who by an act of faith placed their trust in Him alone. To His closest disciples He promised,

> "In my Father's house are many rooms; if it were not so, I would have told you. I am going there to prepare a place for you. And if I go and prepare a place for you, I will come back and take you to be with me, that you also may be where I am" (John 14:2–3).

As an eyewitness to Jesus after Jesus Himself had risen from the dead, the Apostle John explained the purpose for the writing of the Gospel record:

> "Jesus did many other miraculous signs in the presence of His disciples, which are not recorded in this book. But these are written that you may believe that Jesus is the Christ, the Son of God, and that by believing you may have life in His name" (John 20:30–31).

The goal of the Gospel writers was to present evidence for the claims of Jesus that He was who He said He was—God in the flesh—and that He had power to do what He said He could do—give to those who believed in Him eternal life! Earlier in his account of Jesus' life, John had written that verse which even those who know nothing else of the Bible, God's written Word, have probably heard, "God so loved the world that He gave His one and only Son, that whoever believes in Him shall not perish, but have eternal life" (John 3:16).

In the minds of most people, the claims of Jesus began what some call "Christianity." Today Christianity is considered one of many religions competing for converts. Those who believe in Jesus are called "Christians." Yet few people, even within the Church, understand what this religion called "Christianity" is really all about. Most think that other religions have just as much validity as Christianity; they certainly don't consider it to be unique.

Have YOU ever wondered why those who believe in Jesus are called "Christians?" The answer appears to be obvious: Jesus claimed to be the "Christ," the "Messiah." "Christ" is the Greek translation of the Hebrew word, "Messiah," which means "Anointed One." But where did this word or name come from? And what does it mean for us today? What does it have to do with eternal life? These are important questions which we must answer if we are to offer Judaic Christianity as the one and only true religion!

People of every age have pondered the "deep" questions of life. Philosophers have attempted to come up with answers to satisfy the human need for a purpose for our existence, while science has attempted to explain our origin as nothing more than a chance event in an infinite universe. Yet, within the human heart there remains the thought of eternity; of living forever.

Solomon, a man who ruled over the people of Israel some three thousand years ago, wrote these words:

> "God has made everything beautiful in its time. He has also set eternity in the hearts of men; yet they cannot fathom what God has done from beginning to end" (Ecclesiastes 3:11).

Our desire for purpose and for hope beyond the grave arises because we are made in the image of the eternal God who created all things. Most people claim to believe in the existence of "*a*" god. Oh, there are those who stubbornly maintain that Chance rules the universe, but even they borrow truth from the very things they deny. They, too, look for purpose in life—for reasons why things happen; and they, too, look for hope in order to go on toward tomorrow and whatever may lie ahead. No one can live without hope; and that hope, for most people, is that the grave is NOT the final resting place! Even people who know little about God or the Bible want to believe that "heaven," or a place like it, really exists, and that everybody except the really bad people go there. Other religions claim their path or road to paradise and promise their followers a place there.

While the stubborn few deny that ANY God exists, most people confess that there must be a "force," a "god," who oversees the universe. Christians claim to know this God personally, to have an intimate knowledge of Him and His plan for the world and for mankind, but few can answer the most basic questions about Him. Mankind's quest for eternal life results in all kinds of ideas, theories and, yes, religions, as people try to determine who God is, what He is like and what He expects or requires of us in order to pass the test and be counted worthy of eternal life.

So, who is this God whom Christians claim to know? How is the Christian's "God" any different than the "gods" of other religions? Ask a thousand people and you will probably get a thousand answers; but surely there must be a way to arrive at the truth! What if you could KNOW that there IS a God who is real; who created the world and everything in it, including YOU!? What if you could KNOW Him and understand where you came from and why you are here? What if you could KNOW what happens when you die, when you take your last breath? What if you could KNOW that you will live forever in a perfect world, in the very presence of this God??

Sound impossible? Well, I have good news for you—actually, Jesus has good news for you! Shortly before He was put to death by His enemies (we'll explain that later), Jesus was talking with His disciples, His followers, those who had been with Him for somewhere around three years as He had taught about the "kingdom of heaven" and had performed many miracles, and suddenly He looked up and began praying. He said,

> "Father, the time has come. Glorify your Son, that your Son may glorify you. For you granted Him authority over all people that He might give eternal

life to all those you have given Him. Now this is eternal life . . ." (John 17:1–2).

Are you listening to this?? Jesus, this man who claimed to be God in the flesh; who could raise the dead and heal the sick and still the waters—this man who claimed to be the "Christ," the One anointed by God to be King over His people—Jesus is about to give THE definition of eternal life. If you were asked to define eternal life you would probably say that it means, quite simply, "Living forever!" Ah, but there is much more to eternal life than simply existing.

Jesus explained to His disciples:

> " . . . This is eternal life: that they may know You, the ONLY true God, and Jesus Christ, whom You have sent" (John 17:3).

John, the same disciple whom we quoted previously, wrote the following words in a letter to the churches:

> "I write these things to you who believe in the name of the Son of God so that you may KNOW that you have eternal life!" (I John 5:13).

Did you hear that??!! "So that you may KNOW that you have eternal life!" Let me return to my original question: "Do you want to live forever?" Writing this book is much more than an "intellectual exercise" for me; rather, it is a humble attempt to communicate, to those whose minds and hearts God may open, the truth which God Himself, through the centuries, has revealed to those whom He chooses. What follows finds its foundation in the Bible—what those who know Jesus understand to be the very Word of the One, True God.

The Bible is the textbook, the source of all that I hope to share with you. I would expect you to believe nothing of what I say, unless it can be supported by the words of Holy Scripture, which were given by God as His Spirit spoke to the hearts and minds of those who wrote it. The Apostle Paul, a Jewish man who came to believe that Jesus was the promised Messiah, wrote,

> "The holy Scriptures are able to make you wise for salvation through faith in Christ Jesus. All Scripture is God-breathed" (II Timothy 3:15–16).

Peter, a disciple of Jesus, wrote,

> "No prophecy of Scripture came about by the prophet's own interpretation. For prophecy never had its origin in the will of man, but men spoke from God as they were carried along by the Holy Spirit" (II Peter 1:21).

The Bible is unlike any other book in the world. I cannot prove to you that the Bible is the "inspired," God-breathed, Word of the One true God. Many have read it, or at least parts of it, and have remained unconvinced and unmoved by what they read. But no other book has survived the centuries and transformed the lives of millions of people like the Bible has done and continues to do. Those who have come to know the God who reveals Himself in the Bible have found hope and peace and joy and purpose which no other religion offers. While I cannot claim to be "inspired," as were the writers of the Bible, I offer you what follows as one in whom the Spirit of God is at work. I know that there are others who claim to speak truth, who claim that God has spoken to them and given them a "word" for today. I claim no such hotline to God, except that which every true believer in Jesus is given, namely, an understanding of His Word that comes from the work of His Spirit. The Apostle Paul wrote to the church in Corinth about these things and said,

> "I did not come with eloquence or superior wisdom as I proclaimed to you the testimony about God. For I resolved to know nothing while I was with you except Jesus Christ and Him crucified. . . . We have not received the Spirit of the world but the Spirit who is from God, that we may understand what God has freely given us. This is what we speak, not in words taught by human wisdom but in words taught by the Spirit, expressing spiritual truths in spiritual words" (I Corinthians 2:1–2,12–13).

As a pastor for twenty-eight years, God, in His wisdom, has chosen to give to me an understanding of His plan of salvation, His plan to save those who believe from His coming judgment, which seems to be desperately lacking in our world today. You will find nothing unique about what I write on these pages. What I share here has been and continues to be available to anyone who commits himself or herself to studying the Bible and listening to what God says through the inspired writers. As one who has received God's Spirit and studied God's Word, I am compelled to share what God has revealed to me through His Word, namely, that there is ONE true God, ONE true religion, ONE way of receiving eternal life, ONE Savior of mankind, and ONE LORD of the universe!

However, at the same time, I confess my own weakness and my own sin. I encourage you to take nothing of what I may say upon MY authority, for I have no authority except what has been given to me by God Himself to proclaim His Word. I urge you to read and to study the textbook from which I take my thoughts, and upon which the words of this book are founded—the Bible; for therein you will find the truth which will set you free; the truth which will bring to you God's gift of eternal life!

I believe that there IS such truth, and that ordinary people like you and me can understand it and accept it and be transformed by it as the very Spirit of God works within our minds and hearts. "Faith" is NOT something that you have to leap into! True faith is based on knowledge. The Apostle Paul wrote to the Romans, "Faith comes from hearing the message, and the message is heard through the word of Christ" (Romans 10:17). People today are being led astray because they are not able to distinguish truth from falsehood, having no reliable source upon which to depend. Few understand that the Bible is ONE book, ONE story, which traces the hand of the God who created us from the beginning of time until its end.

Many people know bits and pieces of God's Word, which they use to give themselves comfort or to justify certain actions. But few realize that within its pages the Bible holds the key to eternal life and the answers to our deepest questions. By accepting the Bible as the very Word of the One, true God, you and I have within our grasp wisdom that can be found nowhere else.

From the beginning, God has revealed Himself to mankind, and when mankind rebelled against Him and became darkened in their understanding, God did not stop revealing Himself to those whom He chose to give ears to hear. As you will see, all the religions of the world claim to offer truth, yet confusion reigns. How can anyone know what is REALLY true? Most people have given up, or have accepted the lie that there is no absolute truth, that there is some truth in all religions. Even those who claim to use the Bible as their standard for truth fail to fully comprehend the importance of KNOWING that Jesus is "the Way, the Truth and the Life," and that "no one comes to the Father" except through Him! (John 14:6). Instead, they "believe" on the basis of some hard to describe feeling, a feeling which may come and go along with the changing turns of life.

Many who claim to know Jesus, who take the name of "Christian," consider Him to be a ticket to heaven, and know little of who He is or why it was necessary for Him to come. Jesus warned that many will be deceived who think they know Him, but who are not trusting in Him as the Savior—who fail to understand the consequences of sin and rebellion against God. For these, "Christianity" is just a word, the name of their particular religion. There is no understanding of what it means that Jesus is the Christ, the Messiah, and even less concern about whether others believe in Him or know the true God. Like so many before them, they think that by being religious they somehow qualify for eternal life.

And then there are the Jews, those who claim to be "the people of God." The name of their religion is "Judaism." They claim to believe that only the first part of the Bible is the very Word of the One, True God, and they look for the coming of the Messiah (at least those who claim to believe in God look for His coming). But they do not believe that Jesus was the promised One! Those who practice their religion continue to believe that God will send the Messiah, who will establish His kingdom and rule over His people, Israel, forever, but few understand that He has already come!!

In one sense, those Jews who are still awaiting the coming of the Messiah are right; He WILL come to this earth to establish His kingdom forever, and He WILL rule over His people, Israel. But, what some Jewish people, and many others (called "Gentiles" in the Bible), have come to understand is that the Messiah has already come once, and His name is Jesus!! Jesus came to do what no mere human being could do: to reconcile sinful human beings with a holy God; to bring spiritual life to those who are spiritually dead. And YOU can learn who this Jesus is and why He and He alone can give you what you and every other human being longs for: Eternal life!

As we examine the unfolding of God's plan of salvation through the Bible, His written Word, we will see that Christianity was not a new religion which began with Jesus, or one of many religions which have some kernels of truth. We will discover that true biblical Judaism is the foundation upon which Christianity is built; that they are not two different and distinct religions, but the ONE, TRUE RELIGION, revealing the ONE TRUE GOD and His plan to save those who believe and to establish His kingdom in a new heavens and a new earth. We will see that the life and work of Jesus, the Christ, is the fulfillment of all that God had promised from the time He created the first man and woman until Jesus was born. And we will see that God tells us what is yet to come, in words and pictures which are clearer than many have imagined.

God does not play games with the souls of mankind. From the beginning, He has revealed Himself and the way to eternal life with Him. It is only because of sin, disobedience to His Law and rebellion against God, that much of mankind has rejected the truth and accepted the lies of evil spiritual forces which proclaim that there is no truth. Jesus said that if you will believe in Him, "you will know the truth, and the truth will set you free!" (John 8:32).

By understanding God's Word, you will come to know God through His Son Jesus Christ, and through faith in Him, the Holy Spirit—the very mind of God—will give you peace of mind in knowing that your Father in heaven loves you and because of the sacrifice of His Son is willing to forgive you and adopt you as one of His children. As you learn to trust Jesus, you will know that He has given you eternal life as a gift; you will know that nothing can separate you from God's love, not even death!

Knowing that you are going to live forever changes your whole perspective on life; it gives you a peace that passes understanding in the midst of trials, it gives you hope in the midst of the darkest hours, it gives you unspeakable joy as you set your mind on things above where Jesus is seated at the right hand of God the Father, and it gives you the motivation to live as a servant of God during the time you are here on this earth, awaiting, looking forward to His eternal kingdom.

Do you want to live forever? Do you want to be sure that you have eternal life—that you know this Jesus who claims to be the promised Messiah, the giver of Life? May God open your eyes and your heart as you hear the glorious story of His plan to save all who believe in Jesus, His Son.

Chapter 1

RELIGION:
How Many True Religions Can There Be?

"Religion"— the very mention of the word stirs debates unlike perhaps any other word in the English language, or any other language. Most people probably think of religion in terms of having something to do with spiritual things. Religion has to do with belief in a Higher Being, or at the very least, a spiritual world which exists, but about which we know very little. Discussions about religion become very confusing because there is not ONE religion which everyone agrees to be the one and only "true" or "right" one, the one which contains all of the truth necessary for mankind to answer our deepest questions: Where do we come from? Why are we here? Where are we going? What is the purpose of life? Most people agree that there ARE questions which people have which go beyond the understanding we can gain simply from studying the world around us. While some few may still believe that science will someday discover the source of life and therefore be able to answer our questions, after all these years mankind has yet to discover the secrets of the universe. Mankind may be able to take what he finds and produce all kinds of new and interesting things, but only God has ever created anything out of nothing.

Philosophers and others through the centuries have claimed that religion was born out of mankind's attempts to answer these deep questions. While those who teach that man evolved from lower species claim that what we see all around us happened by chance, there remains no evidence that such perfect order ever came out of the chaos which these same people claim existed in the distant past. The uniqueness of the human race can be seen in our quest for meaning and purpose. It is apparent that no other creature has the ability to even ask the questions, let alone answer them. Concern about spiritual matters does not extend beyond the human race. Mankind alone, of all the creatures on the face of the earth, desires to have a sense of purpose, a "raison d'etre," as the French would say—a "reason for being." As a pastor for twenty-eight years, I have seen time after time the awful consequences of people not knowing that there was a reason for their being here in this world. If "Chance" rules, and there is no purpose to tie all of the pieces of our lives together, then despair is sure to follow; and along with doubt and fear, despair displays itself in hundreds of self-destructive behaviors which affect individuals, societies, cultures and nations.

Every day more and more people give up in their search for meaning and join the chorus of voices calling us to "eat, drink and be merry, for tomorrow we may die!" But others continue their search, hoping that by doing so they will finally find the answers that have eluded so many before us; answers that will make sense of this thing we call "Life." There IS, after all, a measure of truth in the statement that the religions of the world were born out of mankind's attempts to answer the deep questions of life. In fact, the various religions of the world ARE mankind's attempts to explain the existence of life and the possibility of life after death. Through the ages people have sought to understand the origin of life and have searched to discover how to achieve immortality. Each culture has devised its gods to explain life and death, good and evil. Virtually every society has established a set of rules or laws by which to govern and control human actions and has offered some type of reward to those who lived according to the standard of goodness established by their particular religion.

Today more and more people have accepted the call for religious tolerance. After all, we are all on this planet together and we need to respect each other's ideas and beliefs. It is not politically correct to say that what someone else believes is false; after all, someone might be offended. Indeed, someone might be offended; indeed, GOD WILL be and IS offended by a religious tolerance which leaves mankind without the knowledge of the One TRUE God who has revealed Himself not only in His creation, but in His written Word and in His own Son, His own Being!!

Where does all of the talk about religion leave us if we only arrive at a place where we accept anything and everything as "POSSIBLE truth?" Are we any closer to finding the "REAL truth" among all the choices which have been set before us? Talk to the true believers of

RELIGION: How Many True Religions Can There Be?

any religion and you will hear them speak with conviction and resolve of what they "know" to be true. Yet, most are content to believe what they simply feel to be true and to allow other people the "freedom" to discover the "truth" for themselves. That sounds rather noble; after all, who am I to force my personal beliefs on you or anyone else? Some even go so far as to make the foolish claim that there is some truth in every religion (as if contradictory ideas can both be true), and that it is up to each person to search the smorgasbord of religions to find what may be true for them. No wonder that some have begun to call the Word of God "TRUE truth." Real truth cannot be different for different people. Truth is always truth, whether some deny it or try to change it; truth remains the same because it comes from the God who does not change.

Any study of the many different religions in the world leads only to confusion. If you are not confused already, you should be! Far from answering the deep questions of life, the discussion carried on by "leaders" and "experts" in the field of religion has left people lost in a whirlpool of ideas which seems to arrive nowhere. Many come to the conclusion that no one knows the "truth" and that all we can do is our best, and hope that is good enough! But, good enough for what?? Must we then guess about such important things? Are we left to ponder, without any hope of arriving at an answer? If there is a "God," or "gods," why do we not have information from the very "Source" which would satisfy our longing to KNOW??

Take heart; we do!! While much of the discussion concerning religion centers around ethics and human behavior—what is right or wrong and how to get people to do what is right—a crucial, indispensable part of the topic appears to be missing, as people argue back and forth about their own particular beliefs. What is missing?? God!! A God who reveals Himself and the truth about you and me that explains our existence and answers our questions. The ancient philosophers determined that there must have been a "First Mover," a "Force" of some kind, which set things in motion so that we have somehow arrived where we are today. Science has discovered certain laws within the universe which control nearly every aspect of life and explain the movements of planets and stars and galaxies and the universe at large. Throughout the ages, religions have recorded mankind's attempts to explain who or what this "God" is, hoping to uncover some formula to discover what some today call "true truth."

Yet, in spite of all of mankind's attempts to answer our questions about life and its purpose, as well as our destiny, the questions remain unanswered and, in the minds of many, unanswerable! But we are not the first to arrive at such an impasse, at such a dilemma. Civilizations which have gone before us have come to similar conclusions and have passed on to future generations only the frustration of searching and never finding the answers. However, for many the search ended nearly two thousand years ago. It was in the city of Athens, a city well-known for its philosophical/religious debates, that a man who claimed to have truth from the One, True God declared to the philosophers of his day a message which offered an explanation of certain events which had taken place shortly before—an explanation which joined together the past, the present and the future into one picture for all to see and understand.

His name was Paul, and he was a Jew; in fact, he was a Pharisee, one of the religious teachers of the Jews. He had persecuted those who had accepted Jesus as the promised Messiah, the One whom the Jews had been looking for since the days of Moses, and even before, the One who would deliver them from their "enemies" and usher in a new and glorious age where God would rule over the whole earth. Not believing that Jesus was this promised One, Paul zealously judged these new followers of Jesus as heretics and had many of them imprisoned, and some even put to death. He believed that they were starting a new religion and that by doing so they were committing the worst kind of heresy and threatening the very fiber of their society. For more than two thousand years the Jews, the descendants of Abraham, had believed in the One, True God, Jehovah, Yahweh. Now some were claiming that Jesus was the Son of God, in fact, that He WAS God, come to earth in the form of a man. They were claiming that this Jesus was the King whom the prophets had predicted God would send to deliver His people; the King who would re-establish the nation of Israel and rule over God's people in Jerusalem. Paul made it his mission to persecute these heretics and to dissuade others from following their false teachings.

But on one of his journeys to persecute Christians, Paul himself had an encounter which would forever change his life. On the road to the city of Damascus Paul, then called by his Hebrew name, Saul, was struck blind by a bright light and Jesus Himself spoke to him, asking why Paul was persecuting Him. Over the next few days, as he lived in total darkness, God revealed to Paul the true light which alone is able to awaken man's soul. Now convinced that Jesus had, indeed, risen from the dead as His disciples had claimed, and that He was the promised Messiah whom the Jews had been looking for because of the prophecies contained in their Scriptures, Paul became a follower of Jesus. He studied the "writings" which he had thought he understood, and was ultimately sent by Jesus and by the early Church to take the Gospel message to all people, not only to the Jews, but also to the Gentiles (the nations).

It was this Paul who came to the city of Athens on one of his missionary journeys. The city of Athens was well-known for its philosophers. The men of the city would sit and discuss the latest ideas, never arriving at a final conclusion, but enjoying the debate—much like many today. As Paul entered the city, he observed the many statues and buildings which displayed the "gods" of the people. In the Greek world, as in cultures which had gone before them, there were many gods, and people were allowed to believe whatever they wanted. How often today do you hear people saying something like this: "People have the RIGHT to believe whatever they want!"??

Into this atmosphere of religious tolerance marched Paul, armed only with what he believed was truth, truth which all people needed to hear. Let me quote for you a bit of what he said as he stood up at the meeting-place for those interested in religious debate. He began,

> "Men of Athens! I see that in every way you are very religious. For as I walked around and looked carefully at your objects of worship, I even found an altar with this inscription: TO AN UNKNOWN GOD" (Acts 17:22–23).

Yes, the people of Athens WERE religious, if what people mean by religious is that they think and talk about God or gods. By that definition, I live in one of the most religious countries in the world!! All around are church buildings, and there are an increasing number of other religions being promoted and explored by many. Even the most primitive societies have been found to be religious, with beliefs to offer those interested enough to examine them, and rules to follow which promise to achieve the desired results. Religious tolerance demands that we allow people to search, to wander, to drift, to meander through the maze of conflicting data and to arrive at their own personal religion.

But listen to what Paul has to say to the men of Athens, and to all who believe that it is their right to decide what is true and what is not true. After noting the religious atmosphere in Athens, and the attempts of the Athenians to cover all their bases by erecting an altar "TO AN UNKNOWN GOD," Paul declares,

> "Now what you worship as something unknown, I am going to proclaim to you" (Acts 17:23).

Paul is claiming to have knowledge which the people in Athens did not possess. In their quest to be all-inclusive, they had omitted some vital knowledge—knowledge which, if believed, would go beyond anything they had discussed or debated before this time—knowledge which could turn their religious world upside down! Without hesitation, Paul continued,

> "The God who made the world and everything in it is the LORD of heaven and earth and does not live in temples built by hands. And He is not served by human hands, as if He needed anything, because He Himself gives all men life and breath and everything else" (Acts 17:24–25).

The Greeks craved "wisdom"; they even had a "goddess" named Sophia (the Greek word for "wisdom"), and they boasted about their insight into spiritual things. This is why this same Paul would later write to the believers in the city of Corinth,

> "Where is the wise man? Where is the scholar? Where is the philosopher of this age? Has not God made foolish the wisdom of the world" (I Corinthians 1:20).

Challenging everything they believed up to this time, Paul began with the first question for which all people need an answer if they are to come to an understanding of life and the purpose of their existence, "Where did we come from?" With unmistakable clarity Paul gives the answer, not offering his own ideas or some possible explanation to mix together with other manmade ideas, but a statement of fact which had been revealed to him by God Himself. He places God where God and only God deserves to be—at the top, at the beginning of any discussion about the deep questions of life.

The Bible does the very same thing; it begins not with mankind, but with God.

> "In the beginning, GOD created the heavens and the earth" (Genesis 1:1).

It is so simple, and yet it is precisely here that most people fail to grasp the truth which would bring the very wisdom that the Greeks and peoples throughout the centuries have sought after and pursued. You see, the problem we have today is that people want to begin with themselves and arrive at the truth. Rejecting the very idea that there is a God who created all things, and denying the necessity for divine revelation, mankind begins with man and searches for God. It should be obvious that such an order of things has not led us to the answers we so desperately seek, but instead has left man believing that HE is God, the "master of his own destiny." Such foolishness should be quickly exposed by anyone thinking rationally, but, as we shall see, that is precisely what man can no longer do!

So, beginning with the bold statement that there is a God who created the world and everything in it, including mankind, Paul goes on to give a very brief, but effective history lesson, explaining God's purpose in creation.

> "From one man He made every nation of men, that they should inhabit the whole earth; and He determined the times set for them and the exact places where they should live. God did this so that men would seek Him and perhaps reach out for Him and find Him, though He is not far from each one of us. 'For in Him we live and move and have our being.' As some of your own poets have said, 'We are His offspring'" (Acts 17:26–28).

Quoting some of their own, Paul masterfully places before them the foundation for all religious truth: GOD, the Creator! There is a reason why the Bible begins, "In the beginning, GOD": because we are incapable of arriving at this knowledge by ourselves!! All the different religions prove that mankind cannot decipher the tracks of our Creator. Man is blind, as we shall soon see, and only by God revealing Himself can any truth be known. Unwittingly, people have sensed this to be true, as Paul quotes some of the writers from Athens as saying. Even as those who claim to be enlightened seek to teach others the things they have come to believe, one wonders whether they are so emphatic because they are trying to convince themselves. When faced with death or questions of "Why?" people must eventually confess, "I don't know!"

In a few brief sentences, Paul reveals the God who created all things, including mankind, and explains that God determines the places and the times for people and nations with one purpose in mind: that some would come to know Him and to worship Him. One old confession, written several centuries ago, states, "The chief end of man is to glorify God and to enjoy Him forever." What a glorious "raison d'etre!" What a glorious reason for being!! God created mankind to know truth—to know HIM! And God created us to find our purpose in loving and serving Him.

Oh, but how few understand?! And what consequence arises from this lack of understanding? Listen again to Paul's challenge to the men of Athens:

> "Therefore, since we are God's offspring, we should not think that the divine being is like gold or silver or stone– an image made by man's design and skill. In the past God overlooked such ignorance, but now He commands all people everywhere to repent. For He has set a day when He will judge the world with justice by the Man He has appointed. He has given proof of this to all men by raising Him from the dead!" (Acts 17:29–31).

Having revealed God as the Creator of all things, as the One who sets the boundaries of the nations and who guides the lives of all people, Paul now connects the plan of this One true God with the

RELIGION: HOW MANY TRUE RELIGIONS CAN THERE BE?

person of Jesus of Nazareth. He claims that God will not overlook ignorance, but rather, will judge those who reject His revelation of Himself and His offer of forgiveness through Jesus, the Christ. There will be a "day of judgment," when all mankind will stand before this God and answer to Him for their rebellion. And the One sitting on the judgment seat will be none other than Jesus, the One scorned by sinful men, the One crucified on a cross, the One mocked as a fool by foolish people who thought they knew the truth about Him, the One who was raised from the dead and who is alive!

Those who thought that Jesus was just a man masquerading as God were wrong! All today who believe that Jesus was a good man who said and did some good things, but who was nothing more than that are equally wrong!! And those who believe that Jesus is dead, who deny His resurrection and ascension into heaven, are also wrong, and have no explanation for the "movement" which continues two thousand years later. By conducting their own search for "truth," rather than beginning with God, people throughout time have deluded themselves into believing that which they know in their deepest being to be a lie: that they are free agents, accountable to no "God," free to believe and to do whatever they wish. However, the Bible, the revelation of truth from the only true God, our Creator, tells us otherwise.

In his letter to the believers at Rome, Paul writes,

> "The wrath of God is being revealed from heaven against all the godlessness and wickedness of men who suppress the truth by their wickedness, since what may be known about God is plain to them, because God has made it plain to them. For since the creation of the world God's invisible qualities–His eternal power and divine nature–have been clearly seen, being understood from what has been made, so that men are without excuse" (Romans 1:18–20).

A thousand years before, David, King of Israel, said the same thing as he wrote Psalm 19:

> "The heavens declare the glory of God; the skies proclaim the work of His hands. Day after day

they pour forth speech; night after night they display knowledge. There is no speech or language where their voice is not heard. Their voice goes out into all the earth, their words to the end of the world" (Psalm 19:1–3).

Yes, the only way to find "absolute truth," truth that is always true, is if the God who created this world reveals it to us. We cannot discover truth on our own. This world did not begin with us; our knowledge is limited, and our ability to understand has been affected by our rebellion against our Creator. But this Creator God has not left us to wonder who He is, or who WE are, and what we are doing here. He has revealed Himself! The debate about religion and which religion is true has a conclusion, for all who want to understand, to all who receive the Spirit of God and who come to Him for truth.

YOU can be one of these people! During my years as a pastor I have had people ask me how I know that Christianity is true. My answer is short and usually not very satisfactory to the one asking the question; but I know they will not understand unless the Spirit of God is at work in them. So, I give them a short answer, stating the truth in a brief way to see if they are really seeking, if they really want to understand. I tell them that I know Christianity to be true because no human being would ever come up with it! No human being would "invent" a religion where God alone is Ruler and where we are His subjects; a religion where God gets all the glory and where human beings are created to serve God. No human being would imagine a religion where all of mankind stands guilty and worthy of judgment, where we can do nothing to please God, to earn His favor, to escape His judgment. No human being would ever devise a plan like that revealed in the Bible, the revelation of God.

And how do I know that? Because they haven't!! Look at all the religions of the world and you will discover that they are all the same! They all have their "roads" or their "paths" to God which include a list of "do's and don'ts" which will hopefully please "God," whoever he or she or it may be. They are all the same; and they all end up in the same place—at uncertainty, doubt and fear. Not one of them explains life or history; and not one of them promises what Christianity promises: eternal life in the presence of a personal, loving, holy, just and merciful heavenly Father. Not one of them offers a "new world," a "new heavens and a new earth," where God Himself will live with those who know and love Him. And not one of them, not one, offers a living Savior like Jesus. The founders of every religion this world has ever known, except one, are dead!!

But I know Christianity to be the only true religion for another reason: Christianity did not begin where most people think it did, with the birth of Jesus and His ministry. No, Christianity began in the Garden of Eden, where God created the first man and woman, and where He gave the first promise of the Savior. We will look at that in the next chapter. What is important to understand from the beginning, when seeking to discover the true religion, is that Christianity is as old as creation, stretching back to the beginning of time. If the religion of the Old Testament part of the Bible is called "Judaism," after the people of Israel, the Jews, then Christianity is Judaism fulfilled. The Jewish Scriptures, the "Old Testament" part of the Bible, point ahead to the coming of the Messiah, the Christ; and the "New Testament" part of the Bible reveals the fulfillment of God's promises to Abraham, Isaac and Jacob, the forefathers of the Jewish nation, Israel. Christianity is the only religion in the world based upon revelation from the God who created all things, revelation which goes from the beginning of the world to its end.

That is what the Bible does; it traces the history of mankind from our beginning in the Garden of Eden, to the end of the age when Jesus returns to establish His kingdom on earth. Though some say that the Bible records "stories" which were made up by men, those who study the Bible with open minds and open hearts see there the unmistakable imprint of the hand and mind of God. For in the pages of holy Scripture God reveals His plan—clearly and openly, for all to see and hear.

Christianity did not just begin when Jesus was born. The birth of Jesus was predicted for centuries before. We shall see that God predicted His birth, His suffering and His coming to build God's kingdom. The failure of most to accept the claims of Christianity today arises from their failure to understand God's plan as it has unfolded throughout time, and as it continues to unfold today. In our modern world, people refuse to accept prophecy; they refuse to believe that there is a God who knows the future as He knows the past. Why?

Because if there is such a God, we must certainly be accountable to Him, and modern man does not want to be accountable to anyone or anything.

Yet in the pages of Scripture, the holy writings of the Bible, we discover a plan that traces God's hand from creation to the birth of Jesus, which explains the present time in which we live and how God is working through those who believe to gather a group of people who will someday live with Him, and which reveals what lies ahead, when Jesus returns to earth, to those who "have ears to hear." From the beginning, when mankind rebelled against God, God promised to send One who would defeat the power of evil, who would suffer in man's place, who would satisfy divine justice and who would give eternal life to those who believed. Why Judaism? Why Christianity? If Christianity is based on Judaism, why are there so few Jews in the Church today? If Jesus was the promised Messiah, the "Anointed One," then why didn't the Jews accept Him when He came? So many questions!

But you CAN understand these things! You CAN know that Jesus IS who He says He is; that He is the very Son of God, "Emmanuel—God with us." You can understand why He came and why He is the ONLY way to have eternal life. God has revealed all these things and more to us through His inspired, God-breathed Word. Remember the words of John, "These things have been written so that you may KNOW that Jesus is the Christ, and that by believing, you may have life in His name" (John 20:31).

There is only ONE TRUE RELIGION!! Since the Bible claims to be true, and it reveals Jesus as the only way to God, either all other religions are false, or Christianity is false. There is no middle ground, no neutral position. Either Jesus is the Son of God who came to suffer and die for our sins and to bring us to the Father, our Creator, or He is a liar and a fraud. Each of us must choose what we will believe. As you read on, I pray that the Spirit of God will open your mind and heart to receive God's truth, the truth revealed in His unchangeable Word, the Bible, and that by believing you may have life in the name of Jesus, our Savior and LORD.

Questions for Reflection:

God created the human race to have a relationship of love with Him. We exist to know God, our Creator, to love Him and to serve Him. In the one true religion God reveals His plan for mankind for all ages.

1. What is the result of not knowing, or of denying the truth revealed in the Bible, the Word of God?

2. Since the religions of the world all contradict each other, how many true religions can there be?

3. When and where did Christianity really begin?

4. Why is it important to know that God has revealed Himself to mankind from the beginning until today?

Chapter 2

MAN'S PROBLEM – GOD'S SOLUTION

That there can be only one TRUE religion makes perfect sense when you begin with God. Since there can be only one Creator, who existed before time and creation, any religion which fails to acknowledge this Creator must be false. Conflicting ideas which contradict each other cannot both be true. The Bible begins with the statement: "In the beginning, God created," and evidence of the Creator is all around us: in the order of the universe, in the purpose found in the smallest of insects or creatures of the sea, in our own bodies and in a million different places and ways. And this One True God continues to reveal His wisdom and His power to mankind, His special creation. When you begin with God, the Creator of the world and everything in it, then you begin to understand your own limitations, and you begin to grasp the truth that we must rely upon His revelation of Himself in order to know Him and to find the purpose for our own lives. Our "destiny" cannot be separated from the God who created us, but must be determined by His will, even as our very existence depends upon Him.

Those who believe in evolution or chance inevitably place their "faith" in things which have far less evidence of their existence than there is evidence of God's existence. For instance, no evidence exists that any species ever changed into another species, yet millions accept this theory as fact. There are many "missing links," not just one, and each one can be explained by accepting the account of creation given in the very first chapter of the Bible, God's revelation. God created the different species according to their own kind, and then He created mankind and gave him a spirit in order that he, and he alone, could communicate with God, his Creator, and have a personal relationship with Him. The difference between mankind and all the other creatures exists not because we have evolved, but because God made us different. We are spiritual beings, made in the image of our Creator.

Believing in "Chance," "Fate" or "Luck" leaves mankind in despair. Many turn to false religions for hope, for insight, for guidance through this thing we call "life." But their lives reveal a lack of contentment and direction which betrays their declarations of "inner peace" and "freedom." If you cannot be sure where you came from, how can you be sure where you are going? Others turn to astrology and horoscopes and the like, searching for anything that will give them hope for tomorrow. Still others boast about the fact that they believe in nothing, not realizing that in so doing they are ascribing to the oldest religion in the world besides the one true religion: the worship of "Self." They have made themselves to be God! They make their own rules and proclaim that they control their own destiny. Such folly hardly merits investigation. And the rest simply go from day to day existing, going through the motions of living, knowing they are missing something but not having a clue where to find it. What a miserable existence!

In your heart, and in the heart of every human being, there is a sense that there is a Creator and that we are here because He placed us here. In his writings, Solomon, the son of David, also a King of Israel, wrote these words: "(God) has set eternity in the hearts of men; yet they cannot fathom what God has done from beginning to end" (Ecclesiastes 3:11). God created us with the insatiable desire to understand the very questions which generation after generation has asked. All the other creatures on this planet live and die and life goes on. All the other creatures on the earth live their lives without questions, without thoughts of where they came from or of tomorrow or life after death. But not mankind!! We have the desire to know more, to understand more, to experience more than we have thus far. That desire comes from the God who created us.

Adam and Eve, the first man and woman God created, knew God intimately. He walked and talked with them in the Garden He had created for them. The theory of evolution did not exist in the Garden of Eden. Adam and Eve knew God as their Creator and lived to enjoy His creation and to care for it. Oh, how they must have enjoyed the beauty around them and the things God taught them! But, all of that changed when Adam and Eve sinned, when they disobeyed God's commands and listened to the lies of Satan. We call this the "Fall," because the whole human race "fell" from God's favor and was affected by the choice which Adam made thousands of years ago. The effects of that choice have been felt throughout the centuries and continue to be felt to this very day. Speaking of the knowledge of God within mankind, Paul explains,

> "Although they knew God, they neither glorified Him as God nor gave thanks to Him, but their thinking became futile and their foolish hearts were darkened. Although they claimed to be wise, they became fools, and exchanged the glory of the immortal God for images made to look like mortal man and birds and animals and reptiles" (Romans 1:21–23).

In the Psalms we read this lament, "The fool says in his heart, 'There is no God'" (Psalm 14:1). Indeed, to deny the existence of God is to give up any hope of knowing the truth which gives life meaning and which leads to eternal life through faith in Jesus Christ. Knowing the Creator is the first step towards spiritual life, towards entering the kingdom of God, towards true freedom from the guilt and power of sin; yet amazingly few are willing to take that step. Why is that true? Why have the majority of people who have ever lived missed the truth? Why have they accepted the lies of other people, when they are left with only confusion, doubts and fears about life and about death and what comes after?

The answer lies in the very beginning of God's Word, in the book of Genesis, the book of "Beginnings." Having created all the creatures according to their "kinds" (species), God created ONE creature to be different than all the rest. He created MAN in His own image. Adam and Eve, the first man and the first woman, were created to know God, to love God and to serve God. They were created to communicate with God, their Creator, and to have a relationship of love with Him. God gave to them the joy of caring for His creation and enjoying His creation. They knew that God was their Creator. They knew the world was His. Where did they acquire this information? From God Himself, the source of all truth. There were no textbooks, no religious "experts," no other people to consult, no opinion polls—just God!

Having created mankind for Himself, God told them to "be fruitful and multiply," and to have dominion over the rest of His creation. They were to rule for God over all that He had made and to use it for His glory, giving thanks to Him for His goodness, wisdom and power. They knew God as loving and powerful and good. Theirs was a perfect world, where there was perfect harmony. There were no lies; there was no sin and no death. Such a world existed at one time. Evolution presents a mindless, heartless "nothing" as somehow evolving over a vast period of time into what we see today. Yet, with all of our modern advances in technology, the human heart remains unchanged. If evolution is true, then we are nothing more than specks in an infinite universe without purpose and without hope beyond the grave. But evolution is not true. In the beginning, GOD created! He created us with the ability to think, to reason, and He created us with emotions so that we could experience love and joy.

God placed Adam and Eve in a special place, the Garden of Eden; and there He placed the "Tree of Life," from which they were free to eat and to fellowship with God. Adam and Eve were physical beings, but they were also spiritual beings. They were created to live forever and to populate the earth. God wanted Adam and Eve to know Him, and as they looked around the Garden God had made for them and saw the beauty and diversity of His creation, they learned more and more about Him. Yet, there was more to learn of their Creator.

In addition to the Tree of Life, God placed there another tree—the "Tree of the Knowledge of Good and Evil." Having been created in God's image, Adam and Eve were like God; they were able to think and to make choices. They knew only what God told them, and they had no reason not to trust Him. God had made all things "very good" and had given Adam and Eve everything they needed to be happy forever. They were loved by their Creator, they lived in a perfect world, they shared God's love with each other and they had communion with God Himself as He walked with them in the Garden.

Some believe all this to be a fairy tale of gigantic proportions, made up to attempt to explain the origin of the human race. Of course, it hardly compares to the "missing link" which some try to establish between "ape-like" creatures and homo sapiens, but you will soon discover that this supposed fairy tale explains all of the bad things which happen in our world today, thousands of years (not millions) later! God created Adam and Eve to know Him and to love Him, AND to serve Him. It was God's purpose to build a "Kingdom"—a physical place in the universe which He had created where He would rule over creatures who were LIKE Him, creatures with a SPIRIT, who would be able to communicate in a very special way with Him, their Creator.

Nowhere else in the universe are there such creatures as mankind! God created the earth in a special way, even as He did the Garden of Eden. Scientists marvel at the composition of the earth and the atmosphere which surrounds it. In our arrogance, we think we have learned so much about the universe since space travel began some fifty short years ago, but we have not even scratched the surface! We are like an infant who thinks he or she has mastered the art of speech when he or she says their first word. Some may remember the first Russian cosmonaut who, having entered into orbit around the earth, remarked, "I did not see God." He must have been blind!! He beheld a sight few human beings have had the privilege of seeing—planet earth from space—and all he could say was, "I did not see God." He saw beauty and majesty and order and gave glory to the creature rather than the Creator, just as the Apostle Paul explained mankind always does. "Claiming to be wise"—ah, how that describes human beings, especially those of us who live today.

God has never left Himself without a witness. Having created mankind it was God's desire to reveal Himself—ALL of Himself—to His special creation. Remember this!! It was, and IS, God's desire to reveal Himself to mankind. Remember what Jesus said to His disciples shortly before His crucifixion: "This is eternal life: that they may know You, the only true God, and Jesus Christ, whom You have sent" (John 17:3). The prophet Jeremiah spoke from the LORD when He wrote,

> "This is what the LORD says, 'Let not the wise man boast of his wisdom or the strong man boast of his strength or the rich man boast of his riches, but let him who boasts boast about this: that he understands and knows me, that I am the LORD, who exercises kindness, justice and righteousness on earth, for in these I delight,' declares the LORD" (Jeremiah 9:23–24).

God desires that people know Him—not just know ABOUT Him—but KNOW Him. And so God placed in the Garden of Eden the "Tree of the Knowledge of Good and Evil." It was placed there not to tempt the man and the woman, but to give them a choice to know God, to trust God and to obey God, their Creator. They required no knowledge except that which God gave them. Therefore, God told Adam and Eve that they could eat of every tree in the Garden EXCEPT the Tree of the Knowledge of Good and Evil. And God told them that IF they ate of that tree they would "die."

If all this is but a fairy tale, then it doesn't make much of a story. In the world we live in today it is predictable that the pair would make the wrong choice. We see people doing that all around us, don't we? We see people making wrong, foolish choices which get them into all kinds of trouble! God has told us in His Word how to live this life and how to find joy and peace, yet we think we are wiser and go our own way; we ignore God's directions, to our own destruction and the harm of others around us. But remember, Adam and Eve had all the information they needed to make the RIGHT choice; they COULD have obeyed God. They could have lived forever in this perfect world; they could have continued in fellowship with God and enjoyed His love, time without end. But they didn't!

Something happened, something which has affected the human race since that time. Actually, the problems began in heaven itself! God had created a "heavenly host," a myriad of spiritual beings which the Bible calls "angels," to serve Him in heaven. The Bible tells us that angels are spiritual beings with "heavenly" or spiritual bodies. And having created mankind, these angels were to be God's messengers to this new world. Though unseen, they would be present and would view the events on planet Earth. And at the command of God they could appear to people and communicate with them. The angels were also able to communicate with God, their Creator, but unlike mankind, they were not physical beings living in a physical world.

In Psalm 8, David writes,

> "When I consider your heavens, the work of your fingers, the moon and the stars, which you have set in place, what is man that you are mindful of

him, the son of man that you care for him? You made him a little lower than the heavenly beings and crowned him with glory and honor. You made him ruler over the works of your hands" (Psalm 8:3–6).

David, and others like him who believed in the one true God, the Creator of the heavens and the earth, understood who God was and so also understood who man was! We are "created beings," made in the image of God, to know and love and serve Him. There is purpose in life, a reason for being beyond mere chance, because God created us with a purpose. Without purpose we are no different than the animals and creatures around us. We are here to glorify God, to honor and serve Him out of love. The same was true of the angels in heaven.

But in the halls of heaven a problem arose: a certain angel, a beautiful creature, with a "spiritual" body or appearance, grew proud. This angel was no longer satisfied to be God's servant; he wanted to be GOD!! How could this be? How could a creature who knew God, who existed in the perfect presence of God, make such a horrible choice? All we know is that, like mankind, God created the angels with the ability to choose; and with the ability to choose comes the possibility of making the wrong choice.

This angel's name was "Lucifer," who later became known as "Satan." The prophet Isaiah writes of him when he says,

"How you have fallen from heaven, O morning star, son of the dawn. You have been cast down to the earth, you who once laid low the nations! You said in your heart, 'I will ascend to heaven; I will raise my throne above the stars of God; I will sit enthroned on the mount of assembly, on the utmost heights of the sacred mountain. I will ascend above the tops of the clouds; I will make myself like the Most High'" (Isaiah 14:12–14).

This beautiful creature, made to serve God in heaven itself, became proud, and through an act of his will, attempted to make himself equal to God. He led a rebellion against God and other angels followed. How utterly foolish, yet not unexpected by God. He could have made the angels and mankind like robots; He could have made them without the ability to choose, but then their love would not have been real. Their service would have been without zeal, without passion, without feeling!! We only feel strongly about what we choose to do. So, God allowed for the possibility of such a rebellion in order that He might reveal Himself in an even fuller, more complete way.

Be reminded again that it is God's desire to reveal Himself to His creation—to those creatures to whom He has given the ability to understand, to communicate, to KNOW truth and to fellowship with Him. But always, at all times, God is in complete control of everything that happens. He could have prevented the rebellion of Satan and the other angels, and He could have prevented what would happen next; but for His own purposes, God determined to allow it and, in fact, to use it for His glory, for His honor!

No wonder that those who come to understand these things respond as did the Apostle Paul when he wrote of them by the inspiration (leading) of the Spirit of God in his letter to the believers in Rome,

> "Oh, the depth of the riches of the wisdom and knowledge of God! How unsearchable His judgments, and His paths beyond tracing out! Who has known the mind of the LORD? Or who has been His counselor? Who has ever given to God, that God should repay him? For from Him and through Him and to Him are all things. To Him be the glory forever! Amen!!" (Romans 11:33–36).

Yes, God knew what was about to happen, and the chain of events that it would put in motion, but in His plan from all eternity He had determined to allow it and then to overcome the effects of this rebellion and so to reveal Himself more fully to His creation. The actions of Lucifer opened the door to all the evil we see in the world around us. Though God maintained control over all things and had already devised a plan to overcome what Satan would do, the responsibility for all the evil in the world lies at the feet of Satan and those angels who followed him, AND those from the human race who would yield to his temptations and refuse God's offer of forgiveness and life. What happened in the Garden of Eden that affects you and me today?

Following his rebellion in heaven, Satan determined to build a kingdom of his own to rival God's kingdom. Where God's kingdom was filled with joy and love, Satan thrived on power and greed. As a powerful spiritual being, Satan had been given power unknown on the earth except by God. And so he came to the Garden, continuing his attempt to establish a kingdom where HE could rule, a kingdom which would ultimately overshadow God's kingdom. Where better to begin, he must have thought, than with God's special creation, mankind. If he could get Adam and Eve to follow him, then God's plan to build a kingdom on the earth where people would know and love and serve Him would be overthrown!

Knowing what God had said to Adam and Eve, Satan came to Eve while she was alone and began to question her: "Did God really say, 'You must not eat from any tree in the Garden?'" He began to place doubt, where before there was only trust. He took the one prohibition which God had given to Adam and Eve, and he directly challenged God's authority and truthfulness. He said,

> "You shall NOT surely die; for God knows that when you eat of it (the Tree of the Knowledge of Good and Evil) your eyes will be opened, and you will be like God, knowing good and evil" (Genesis 3:4–5).

Both Adam and Eve had heard God's command that they could eat of every tree in the Garden except the Tree of the Knowledge of Good and Evil. They had no need to eat of this tree. They received all the knowledge they needed directly from God, their Creator. They were already like God; they need not learn of evil or ever know of its disastrous consequences. They had fellowship with God, their Creator. Everything was perfect! But Adam was apparently otherwise occupied and at that moment Eve was alone and she made a fatal error: she decided to question what God had revealed to her. She decided to think for herself, ignoring God's revelation. She decided to operate on the basis of information which she had no way of "checking out," to see whether it was true or false. So she ate of the fruit of the forbidden tree, and also gave some to Adam, her husband.

Immediately, things changed. Some people, failing to understand that mankind is a spiritual being, as well as a physical being, question whether God's threatened punishment was carried out, claiming that God had said that in the day that Adam and Eve disobeyed they would die, yet they obviously continued to live. But, Adam and Eve DID die; they died spiritually; they became unable to obey God as they had before. Further, they became unable to have communion with God, for now they were afraid of His punishment. They had "sinned," they had "missed the mark" of perfection which God requires of those with whom He will fellowship, with whom He will live.

Adam and Eve tried to hide from God, and they covered their nakedness with leaves from the fig tree. Fear came into their hearts and their minds. Indeed, they knew and felt things which were new to them. Their eyes WERE opened, as Satan had promised, but they did NOT become like God in only KNOWING good and evil, they actually BECAME evil!! They lost their ability to love, honor and serve God with a willing heart. They became spiritually DEAD, and were thus separated from God, their Creator. And from that moment on, they began to die physically as well. God cursed creation and the ground began to bring forth weeds and thorns, and the animal kingdom would also fight against mankind.

God had made Adam the representative of the human race, and as our representative his actions and the consequences of them were passed on to you and to me. While psychologists and sociologists and anthropologists and other "experts" attempt to explain the thoughts and actions of people, this one act explains the problem mankind faces. You and I see the effects of Adam's choice all around us. The Apostle Paul explains the consequence of Adam's sin when he writes,

> "Sin entered the world through one man, and death through sin, and in this way death came to all men, because all sinned" (Romans 5:12).

As our first representative, Adam determined the future of the whole human race. When he sinned against God, his Creator, his very nature became sinful, indeed, "dead" to God's original design. Every child ever born into this world has inherited this dead, sinful nature. Look around! Can you deny that you see the consequence of mankind's rebellion against God?? But, God IS in control. While He could have stopped the rebellion of the angels and the fall of mankind into sin, God had determined that He would allow it to take place in order that He might more fully reveal Himself to those whom HE would choose.

How could this possibly serve God's ultimate purpose: to reveal Himself to mankind? How could God recover from this rebellion, first by the angels, and now by mankind? As He had done with Satan, God now cast the man and the woman out of the Garden, knowing that if they ate of the "Tree of Life" in their present condition, they would live forever in a sinful state, separated from Him, living forever in fear and dying without hope of eternal life.

Ah, but God had a plan!! God is "sovereign"; He rules over ALL things and is in control of ALL things. God is never caught by surprise! While He allows His creatures the ability to make choices, He has the wisdom and the power to overrule those choices, and to overrule the negative consequences of those choices, for His own purposes and glory. The prophet Isaiah, urging the people in his day to turn from their sinful ignorance to believe in the true God, writes,

> "Seek the LORD while He may be found; call on Him while He is near. Let the wicked forsake his way and the evil man his thoughts. Let him turn to the LORD, and He will have mercy on him, and to our God, for He will freely pardon. 'For my thoughts are not your thoughts, neither are my ways your ways,' declares the LORD. 'As the heavens are higher than the earth, so are my ways higher than your ways and my thoughts than your thoughts'" (Isaiah 55:6–9).

Because of his sin Adam could no longer obey God; he was spiritually "dead." He was "bent" towards evil. The same is true of every human being who has walked upon this earth since the beginning, except for one, Jesus. Look around and claim that this isn't so when people of all walks of life cry out, "What makes people do the things they do?!"

So few today understand the condition of the human heart from a spiritual perspective. People try to explain sin by blaming it on a child's environment or lack of education or negative influences from society. All of these things may contribute to the choices a person makes, but the Bible, God's Word, His revelation, clearly explains the problem we have. We are born, now, as every human being since Adam and Eve has been born, with what the Bible calls a "sinful nature." It is not "just" that we are ignorant; it is that we are in active rebellion against our Creator. We "suppress the truth" in unrighteousness; we deny that such a God exists; we make ourselves out to be "God" and devise our own religions and our own methods to please the gods we make up in our minds and hearts. Mankind, including every man, woman, boy and girl, is LOST!! We are destined to face the judgment of the God we claim does not exist—the God who is loving, compassionate and merciful, but also holy and just and truthful.

The prophet Jeremiah writes, "The heart is deceitful above all things and beyond cure. Who can understand it?" (Jeremiah 17:9). David writes in Psalm 14,

> "They are corrupt, their deeds are vile; there is no one who does good. The LORD looks down from heaven on the sons of men to see if there are any who understand, any who seek God. All have turned aside, they have together become corrupt; there is no one who does good, not even one" (Psalm 14:1–3).

And the Apostle Paul adds to this refrain as he quotes these words hundreds of years later:

> "All have sinned and fall short of the glory of God" (Romans 3:23).

Oh, how people want to believe that this is not true!! As one book written some decades ago proclaimed, people want to believe that, "I'm O.K., You're O.K.!" The very fact that such a book was written reveals that people know that they are NOT O.K., but they are trying to convince themselves otherwise! All is NOT well with mankind! There was a time when some believed that the human race would eventually evolve into a golden age, a "utopia," where everyone would be loving and kind and where there would be no more disease or death, where people would live at peace with one another and with creation.

Few are so optimistic today! Instead, we see around us the truth of mankind's spiritual death and the horrible consequences of that first choice made so long ago by Adam, our representative. In his letter to the church at Ephesus, Paul writes, "You were DEAD in your transgressions and sins . . . by nature objects of wrath. . . . without hope and without God in the world" (Ephesians 2:1,3,12).

Such became the state of mankind immediately after he had sinned against God in the Garden of Eden. The consequences were immediately evident: Adam and Eve had children and one of their sons, Cain, killed his brother, Abel, because he was jealous and angry—emotions which arose because of sin in his heart. Theirs was the first dysfunctional family! Sin always causes us to think of ourselves and what WE want, rather than upon God and what HE wants. As mankind multiplied upon the earth, God looked down from heaven and saw how great man's wickedness on the earth had become, and that "every inclination of the thoughts of his heart was only evil all the time" (Genesis 6:5). And we read that "the LORD was grieved that He had made man on the earth, and His heart was filled with pain" (Genesis 6:6).

Yes, God has feelings and emotions. He is not weak as we are in our sin; His emotions do not control His actions, but He does feel—otherwise, how could He love?? But would God's purpose be overcome by Satan's temptation of Adam and Eve, and their ultimate disobedience? Would God have a kingdom over which He would rule; where people, His special creation, would know, love and serve God, their Creator??

There was never any doubt!! For in the Garden of Eden, before Adam and Eve were even cast out lest they eat of the Tree of Life, God pronounced His curse upon Satan with the first promise of a Savior— One who would bring deliverance, "salvation," to those who would believe on Him. God said to Satan, the serpent,

> "Because you have done this, cursed are you above all the livestock and all the wild animals! You will crawl on your belly and you will eat dust all the days of your life. And I will put enmity between you and the woman, and between your offspring and hers; He will crush your head and you will strike His heel" (Genesis 3:14–15).

God was saying, "Satan, you will not win. You will not have the last word; you will not succeed in your rebellion. You and yours will be defeated, and My kingdom WILL be established on the earth." The rest of the Bible reveals God's plan to "save" mankind from the just consequences of our sin—eternal death! Why is Christianity the only true religion? Because no other religion in the world deals with man's worst problem: separation from God! All the other religions of the world focus on man's attempts to "save" himself, to conquer the "urges within," to overcome the evil in our world.

But in the Old Testament Scriptures we will see how God began to unfold HIS plan—a plan forged in the mind of God before the world was even created—God's plan to reveal Himself to those whom He would choose from a fallen human race and to save them from the judgment they rightly deserved. It was, and is, God's desire to reveal Himself to those who have "ears to hear," who receive His Spirit and who believe in HIS Savior, the promised One, the "Offspring," the "Seed" of the woman. God would reveal Himself as a loving, compassionate, forgiving and merciful God, but also as a holy, just and righteous God, worthy of our praise and worship.

Search, study, read the history and the writings of every other religion in the world and you will find none—not one—which provides the solution to our "sin problem." While some think that Christians are always trying to make people feel guilty, the truth is that all people ARE guilty before a holy and just God who created them. There are NO exceptions!! Denying the truth never changes the truth. Whether in the Old Testament Scriptures or the New, the Bible tells us that we will one day stand before God, our Creator.

Solomon writes in Ecclesiastes, writing about all the different ideas of what gives purpose to life,

> "Here is the conclusion of the matter: Fear God and keep His commandments, for this is the whole duty of man. For God will bring every deed into judgment, including every hidden thing, whether it is good or evil" (Ecclesiastes 12:13–14).

In his second letter to the church in Corinth, the Apostle Paul wrote,

Questions for Reflection:

While mankind faces many problems on planet earth, our worst problem is sin and its consequences. If we don't understand our real problem we will never arrive at a solution.

1. By denying the existence of the one true God who created us, who or what ultimately takes God's place?

2. How do the first three chapters of the Bible explain the origin of evil in God's perfect creation?

   According to the Bible, explain the condition of the human heart.

   What promise did God make in the Garden of Eden which pointed to a solution to mankind's real problem?

> "We must all appear before the judgment seat of Christ, that each one may receive what is due him for the things done while in the body, whether good or bad" (II Corinthians 5:10).

The writer to the Hebrews adds his voice to the refrai[n] he says,

> "Man is destined to die once, and after that to face judgment" (Hebrews 9:27).

The only true religion began in the Garden of Eden [when God] revealed Himself not only as the God of Creation, but also as [the God of] Salvation—the God who offers life to those who are dead, [life] to those who are worthy of eternal death. By refusing to ac[cept] mankind's problem, the majority of people in the world [reject] God's solution. As we will see, though the Old Testamen[t books] form the basis of true "Judaism," even the majority of Je[ws] rejected the promised Savior when He came because the[y were look]ing for something else. They thought their worst prob[lem was that] they were under the rule of the Roman Empire, but i[n doing so they] overlooked their own hearts.

They had grown callous to God's voice throug[h the prophets] calling them back to Him. They had worshiped idols [and turned] away from the only true God, their Creator. But God v[owed to establish His] kingdom; nothing would stand in His way. His plan W[ould come to] pass, and all who would believe on the Savior would [be forgiven of] their sins and receive the gift of eternal life. How w[ould they know?] The answer lies in only one place—the place where [God has] revealed the truth, the whole truth and nothing but [the truth—the] Bible, the very Word of the One True God!

If you will open your heart and mind to Go[d, He will] show you things that a child can understand, but wh[ich those who are] "wise in their own eyes" pass by as foolishness. [May God bless] you as you hear more from His Word; may He give [you understanding] and turn your heart towards Jesus, the promised S[avior who] came to save ALL who believe from their sins a[nd give them the] gift of eternal life!!

Chapter 3

"The Covenant of GRACE"

Since religion deals with spiritual matters, any religion which claims to be the only TRUE religion must certainly answer the deep spiritual questions which mankind proposes. People ask all kinds of questions of religious people, foremost among which are questions about suffering and evil. Beginning with man and our limited perspective, people put GOD on trial, as it were, and demand that HE give THEM the answers they seek. The gods of the myriad of religions offered by man are impotent gods, restricted in their ability to solve mankind's problems. No one really expects these gods to fix the world's problems or to answer our questions. But people seem to expect more out of Christians for they are forever asking us to explain how God can allow suffering and tragedy to take place. Why do they ask such questions of Christians, but not of other religions? The answer is obvious: it is because the God who reveals Himself in the pages of the Bible claims to be different; He claims to be omniscient (knowing all things), omnipotent (all-powerful), and omnipresent (present everywhere). If this is the case, then why doesn't He DO something about our problems??!!

Of course, such a question fails to grasp mankind's worst problem: SIN—rebellion against this God who rules over all things; a rebellion which has resulted in separation from fellowship with God, our Creator and which has left each of us spiritually dead and blind. What the human mind WILL NOT accept is that because of sin we deserve nothing good from God. Rather, the writers of Scripture tell us that "the wages of sin is death" (Romans 6:23). You and I have earned spiritual and physical death—the result of being separated from God, who is Life. WE are responsible for the suffering which exists in the world today! By rejecting the One True God and going our own way, we have reaped what we have sown! While people today do everything they can to escape responsibility for their choices, deep down we all must confess our sins, our weaknesses, our attempts to play God with our lives. Self sits on the throne of the hearts and minds of those who have not come to know their Creator. People do not only have problems in this world, people ARE the problem!! God would be perfectly just in condemning every man, woman and child to eternal death. That is what we deserve; that is what we have earned.

Remember what the poets of Athens in ancient Greece had written: "In 'him' we live and move and have our being." Those who reject God live on borrowed time, with each breath they take receiving the gift of physical life from God without acknowledging Him or giving thanks to Him. Thus, those who do not know Him increase their guilt moment by moment, for God knows their minds and sees their hearts. In the third chapter of John's Gospel account he writes that now famous verse, John 3:16, and then, going on, explains the state of mankind:

> "For God so loved the world that He gave His one and only Son, that whoever believes in Him shall not perish but have eternal life. . . . Whoever believes in Him is not condemned, but whoever does not believe stands condemned already because he has not believed in the name of God's one and only Son" (John 3:16,18).

Religion which begins with man always ends with a god made in man's image: a god with limited wisdom and limited power. Mankind cannot, WILL not imagine a God to whom we must be accountable. We want a God who will serve US, who will be there when we call and otherwise leave us to our own desires. But when we begin with God, we find the God whose wisdom and power are unlimited—a God who is able to give us precisely what we need most: a Savior, a Deliverer, One who can lead us back to Him and who can open the door to God's kingdom for those who are lost! And you and I ARE lost, desperately lost, until or unless we come to know the truth about ourselves and about God. Even those who have never heard of God, who have learned of other gods, and who follow other religions are responsible for their rejection of God.

We read in Paul's letter to the Romans this explanation:

> "The wrath of God is being revealed from heaven against all the godlessness and wickedness of men who suppress the truth by their wickedness, since what may be known about God is plain to them, because God has made it plain to them. For since the creation of the world God's invisible qualities–his eternal power and divine nature–have been clearly seen, being understood from what has been made, so that men are without excuse" (Romans 1:18–20).

People through the ages have begun their search with themselves and have created gods who are not worthy of worship, gods who cannot solve our problems or change our hearts. The one, true God, our Creator, has the right to judge us and the power and authority to carry out that judgment. The Bible could have ended after the first three chapters: God created everything good, but Adam and Eve sinned against Him and He cast them out of the Garden. Thus separated from God, man lived in sin all his days and faced physical and spiritual death. The End!! God would have been perfectly just in condemning all of mankind to such a fate. We deserve it; we earned it!! But the Bible doesn't end there, praise God! As you read the Bible, and as you read the following pages, you will see how God reveals Himself as a just and holy God, as well as a loving, compassionate and gracious God. He is not one or the other; He is both!

Though God was grieved when He saw the spiritual state of mankind, His intention was to build a kingdom on the earth, this planet! Satan would NOT win!! Rather, in His eternal wisdom God had already determined to turn the evil which Satan tried to do to work out for His glory, and for the good of those who would believe in the coming Savior. God had already planned to save mankind from spiritual death, even before Adam and Eve gave in to Satan's temptation. In his letter to the church in Ephesus the Apostle Paul would explain that those who believe in Jesus were chosen in Christ "before the creation of the world" (Ephesians 1:4). And if we follow closely through Scripture as God unfolds His plan, we will begin to grasp why God allowed sin to enter the world and, ultimately, allowed His own Son, Jesus, to be crucified in our place.

But first we must become familiar with a word which all who know the true God come to love: GRACE. Man-made religions know nothing of grace; they only lead mankind ever deeper into a maze of religious gymnastics designed to earn the worshiper a place in "paradise." Always, the "life-after-death" which is being offered must be earned by those who by their very nature are unable to keep all of the rules which are imposed by the so-called leaders or founders of these various religions. But the Bible introduces us to the God of Grace—the God who knows the sinful heart of mankind and its disastrous effects throughout the entire human race, and yet, who loves His special creation and desires true communion/fellowship with people just like you and me.

GRACE means, quite simply, "undeserved favor." You cannot earn grace, for if you could, it would no longer be grace. By definition, grace must be received as a gift, without any payment by those who receive it. The message of the Bible, and thus of Christianity, is that God provides a way for sinful human beings to be forgiven and restored to the original state in which Adam and Eve were created, in righteousness and true holiness, and then God invites such human beings to live with Him forever in a new heavens and a new earth. In a nutshell, that is what the Bible is really all about!

No other religion, NOT ONE, offers such a thing! No other religion reveals the God of Grace as He is—loving, kind, good and compassionate, yet holy, righteous and just. But in the Bible God reveals His full character. After Adam and Eve had been cast out of the Garden of Eden, God did not leave them totally, nor did He forget about them. Adam and Eve had children and they worshiped God. Two of their sons, Cain and Abel, are mentioned in Genesis 4. They had apparently been instructed in worship as they both brought offerings to God. Already, God had instructed Adam and Eve and their offspring that a sacrifice must be offered for sin; blood had to be shed in order to "atone," or "pay for," mankind's rebellion against God—in order to satisfy His justice.

Abel brought a lamb as his sacrifice, and God received his sacrifice and showed Abel His favor. But Cain brought some of the crops which he had produced as an offering to the LORD. God did not look with favor on Cain's offering and somehow made it plain to Cain that He was not pleased with him. Revealing the sinful nature within him,

Cain did not confess his own sin, that he had ignored God's instructions for bringing an offering. Instead, he became jealous of Abel and allowed his anger to control him, eventually killing his brother.

Now, what was the big deal, some might wonder? The big deal was Cain's heart! He wanted to do things HIS way, which is the fountain of all sin against God. Cain chose to ignore God's instructions that required blood to be shed, and he attempted to come to God by his own efforts and by his own methods. How many do the same thing today?!! Not only in other religions, but in churches throughout the world, people attempt to come to God by their own works, in their own way. Countless millions appear to believe that by simply believing that some god exists, or by going to church, praying and reading the Bible, or by simply being good, they have earned immortality— eternal life. Surely the God who made us wants to live with us and will be satisfied with the little tidbits of devotion which we offer Him. Does that sound sarcastic? Imagine how it looks to the one, true God!! Such an approach didn't work for Cain, and it doesn't work today.

There is only ONE way to come to God and that is GRACE! God WANTS people to come to Him; He wants to forgive and to be reconciled to mankind. Yet, because God is holy, He cannot just overlook our sin, our "uncleanness." His justice must be satisfied; sin must be "paid for!" How can you or I pay for our sin? How can we make it up to God? We continue to sin against Him in our thoughts and words and deeds, and so become more and more guilty. Not a day goes by that we do not sin against the holiness of God, our Creator. We make resolutions, we try to be better, but we do not have the power in ourselves to be perfect, which is what God requires. Perfection is out of our reach as sinful human beings. And because He is holy, God cannot lower His standard, nor can He "grade on the curve," as many would like Him to do. Those who think that God has changed His requirements from the Old Testament days need to read the words of Jesus in the Sermon on the Mount. Jesus explains that mere outward obedience does not fulfill the Law of God, for He sees the heart. And He summarizes God's requirements by saying, "Be perfect, as your heavenly Father is perfect" (Matthew 5:48). God knows that we CAN'T be perfect, yet His holiness will not allow Him to accept anything less. This is precisely why the Bible says that we are LOST; because the human heart, dead in sin, cannot fix itself. We need to be saved; we need to be transformed, from the inside out! In his letter to the believers in Rome the Apostle Paul wrote,

> "The mind of sinful man is death, . . . the sinful mind is hostile to God. It does not submit to God's law, nor can it do so. Those controlled by the sinful nature cannot please God!" (Romans 8:6–8).

That was Cain's problem, and that is OUR problem! As the human race multiplied upon the earth God looked down upon them and saw that every one of the thoughts of man's heart was evil all the time (Genesis 6:5). He was grieved (remember, God has feelings!), and He determined to destroy mankind from the face of the earth. But God did not forget His plan, nor did He abandon His intention to establish His kingdom on the earth. One man, Noah, found favor, GRACE, in God's sight.

God determined to save this one man and his three sons and their families from His judgment upon the earth. God instructed Noah to build an ark because He was going to send a flood upon the whole earth, and through them and their descendants to carry out His plan. Evidence of such a cataclysmic event abounds all over the earth to this day, though science has tried to explain it by offering theories of vast billions of years causing dramatic changes over the face of the planet. Many are interested in the search for Noah's ark, as though it was a Hollywood movie, but these events are real. This planet and all the people on it, except Noah and his family, WAS destroyed by a flood—a global catastrophe sent by God as judgment upon the human race. The Bible records the history of mankind in order to reveal the true state of mankind: bent toward evil and separated from God.

Though God would have been just in destroying the entire human race, He had promised that the "Seed" of the woman would crush Satan's head and restore mankind to communion with his Creator. Therefore, God saved Noah and his family and through them the human race had, in a sense, a new beginning. Why the flood? Why such horrible destruction?? So that those who would come afterwards would know that God is just and holy; so that they would look to God for help and long for a Savior!

More than two thousand years later the Apostle Peter would warn his readers that they should not take God's patience for granted, thinking perhaps that God is really not going to destroy the earth or bring judgment upon mankind as the Scriptures say. And he uses the flood in the days of Noah as an illustration of God's righteous judgment, explaining that this present world is reserved for fire, on that day when God sends the final judgment upon those who have rebelled against Him and who have rejected His offer of forgiveness and life (II Peter 3).

However, as we shall see as we look through the history of Israel in the Old Testament Scriptures, mankind has often ignored God's warnings! It was not long after the flood that the descendants of Noah once again challenged God's authority. God had commanded Noah and his sons to multiply and to spread out over the earth. But their descendants had a better idea! A group of them decided to establish their own kingdom and to make a name for themselves. They began to construct a huge tower which could be seen for miles and miles—a tower that would reach up into the sky.

At this time there was one language among the people of the earth. As God once again looked down upon mankind, He knew that they would continue to turn away from Him, to go their own way, to attempt to build their own world where God would no longer exist. But they would fail! They would live and die and face God's judgment, because their spirits were already dead. They would live forever in spiritual death, for being made like God, our spirits are eternal—they do not cease to exist—neither are they "reincarnated," which means, "given flesh again." When a person dies, his or her spirit lives on, either in the presence of God or separated from God forever. There is no in between!

Therefore, God "confused the languages" of those who were working to build the tower, and because they could no longer communicate, the building stopped and the people scattered over the earth as God had commanded them to do. The first eleven chapters of the Bible explain where we came from, who we are, the existence of evil, the beginnings of the nations and of languages, and the character of the One, True God, our Creator. They also reveal God's wisdom and power, and the foundation for His plan to "redeem," to "pay for" mankind through the sacrifice of One who would come: the "Seed" of the woman, who would crush the head of the serpent, Satan, God's enemy and ours.

No other religion explains the origin of sin and of all of mankind's struggles and trials. In refusing to acknowledge God and to submit to His rule over us, the entire human race continues to experience the consequences of living in rebellion against God. The prophet Jeremiah speaks of the human heart as "desperately wicked," and beyond understanding. Listening to the news of events around the world, we often wonder, "Why do people behave like they do?" The answer lies in the very nature of mankind, living in spiritual death, separated from our Creator. No other religion confronts mankind with the awful truth of our condition. We live "without God and without hope" (Ephesians 2:12) in the world which God created good. We have no one to blame but ourselves.

Ah, but this is NOT the end of the story!! The God of Grace; the God who saved Noah and His family; the God who promised to send a Savior who would destroy evil and Satan, the Tempter, the accuser of mankind; the God who desires to build His kingdom and to live with His special creation, mankind—THIS God, the ONLY TRUE GOD, begins to unfold His plan, a plan devised in the mind of God before He even created the world or mankind. He calls another man, a man named Abram, to believe in Him and to obey Him.

Up until now God had dealt with the entire human race, revealing the depth of mankind's fall into their sinful condition and the extent of their separation from God, their Creator. In the flood and in the confusing of their languages and the scattering of the people over the earth, God displayed His holiness and justice, AND His grace and compassion. Now, God would begin to reveal His PLAN to gather a "people" for Himself; a group of people who would accept His rule over their lives and who would live to worship and serve Him; a people who would love God and who would desire to live with God forever.

Where would God find such a people? All men were sinners; all deserved God's judgment. Yes, but God had a plan, remember? And God has the wisdom and the power to bring His plan to pass, no matter what man or Satan and his demons do. God's plan WILL come to pass.

He begins with Abram, a descendant of Noah's son, Shem. God appeared to Abram and told him to leave his country, his people and his father's house, and to go to a place that God would show him (Genesis 12:1). Abram lived in an area near what is now the Persian

Gulf, not far from where the Bible indicates that the Garden of Eden was.

God said to Abram,

> "I will make you into a great nation and I will bless you. I will make your name great, and you will be a blessing. I will bless those who bless you, and whoever curses you I will curse; and all peoples on earth will be blessed through you" (Genesis 12:2–3).

God's promises to Abram pointed to the future, to a time when the whole world—all peoples, all nations—would be affected by the "seed" of Abram. Though Abram and his wife, Sarai, had no children, God promised him that his descendants would be like the stars of the sky and the sand of the seashore—beyond number! God promised Abram that his descendants would be God's people, and that God would be their God.

We read that Abram believed God and that he obeyed God. He left his country and his people and his father's house and journeyed to the place God showed him—the land of Canaan (what is today, Israel). God said to Abram,

> "I will establish my covenant as an everlasting covenant between me and you and your descendants after you for the generations to come, to be your God and the God of your descendants after you. The whole land of Canaan, where you are now an alien, I will give as an everlasting possession to you and your descendants after you; and I will be their God" (Genesis 17:7–8).

God's covenant with Abram is called the "Covenant of Grace." Abram did nothing to earn God's favor or to initiate fellowship with God. GOD chose Abram, and on the basis of His own wisdom, plan and power, determined to bless him. That is GRACE!! Undeserved favor!! Much later, the Apostle Paul would write to the believers in Ephesus the words which every believer today cherishes:

> "For it is by grace you have been saved, through

faith–and this not from yourselves, it is the gift of God–not by works, so that no one can boast" (Ephesians 2:8–9).

Grace leaves no room for boasting, but only for humbly giving thanks. No one can say when they have come to God, "Look what I have done!" As God chose Abram and made His covenant with him, so those who come to believe in Jesus Christ have also been chosen by God Himself and shown His favor, His grace. We will talk more about how to know that you are one of God's chosen people, but first, we must understand how God fulfilled His promises to Abram and what that has to do with us today.

As we have seen, Abram and Sarai had no children. More than that, Abram was seventy-five years old when God told him to leave his country and to go to Canaan. Years passed, and Abram and Sarai had not had any children and Sarai had begun to doubt God's promise. She convinced Abram that God needed a little help in providing him an heir, so she told him to sleep with her servant and thus have a child and build a family through her. Abram reveals his own sinfulness when he agrees with Sarai and eventually has a son through Sarai's servant, Hagar.

However, God quickly shows Abram that this son, Ishmael, is NOT the promised "seed!" He comes to Abram, now ninety-nine years old, and tells him that his wife, Sarai, who is ninety years old, will have a son. In fact, to make His point clear to Abram, God changes his name to Abraham, meaning, "father of many." God also changes Sarai's name to Sarah, for through her son she would be the mother of nations. God would do what seemed impossible to man, so that when it happened, the glory would go to God!

According to God's promise, Abraham and Sarah had a son, and they named him Isaac, which means, "laughter," because when Sarah heard God's promise she laughed, thinking she was too old to have a baby. Of course, under ordinary circumstances she WAS too old; but God goes far beyond what appears to be ordinary to you and me. God has a plan! God has a purpose in everything He does. History does not go around in unending circles; history is a continuous line stretching from creation to consummation, beginning to end, eternity past to eternity future.

With Abraham, God began the fulfillment of His promise to all mankind when He cursed Satan and promised a Savior. From Abraham's descendants God would bring this Savior into the world, and all who believed in Him would have eternal life. We are told that Abraham believed God's promises and God "credited" Abraham's faith to his account (Genesis 15:6). In other words, by believing God's promises, Abraham accepted God's grace. He admitted that he could do nothing on his own to earn God's favor, God's blessings, and he confessed his dependence upon God to keep His promises. Such is the nature of the faith which God Himself gives to His chosen people; not faith in ourselves, but faith in the God who makes promises and keeps them!!

According to His promises, the rest of the book of Genesis, the first book of the Bible, explains how God makes out of Abraham's descendants a great nation. Isaac, the son of Abraham and Sarah, marries Rebekkah. She gives birth to twins, Jacob and Esau. Though Esau was born first, once again God reveals His sovereign choice, and chooses Jacob, the younger, as the one from whom the promised Savior will come.

God renewed His promises with Isaac, and then with Jacob, promising to be the God of their descendants and to give them the land of Canaan. Jacob has twelve sons, and though he struggles with his old nature of sin, Jacob comes to believe in the true God, the God of his father, Isaac, and his grandfather, Abraham. As He had done with Abraham and Isaac, God promises to make a great nation of the descendants of Jacob. Once again, God reveals Himself as the God who is at work in all the details of life when He changes Jacob's name to Israel, meaning, "He struggles with God." Jacob had come through deep inner struggles to find God to be faithful and trustworthy.

From Jacob would come the nation of Israel, twelve "tribes," a nation created BY God, FOR God; a nation from whom the Savior of mankind would come. Much later, after this nation had grown to more than a million people, having been enslaved in Egypt for four hundred years, Moses would write,

> "The LORD did not set His affection on you and choose you because you were more numerous than other peoples, for you were the fewest of all

peoples. But it was because the LORD loved you and kept the oath He swore to your forefathers that He brought you out with a mighty hand and redeemed you from the land of slavery, from the power of Pharaoh King of Egypt. Know therefore that the LORD your God IS GOD!" (Deuteronomy 7:7–9).

There it is!! The God of Israel; the God of Abraham, Isaac and Jacob; HE is God; the ONLY True God, the Creator of the heavens and the earth! And the only way to know Him is to accept His revelation of Himself. Mankind cannot come to know God in any other way. Beginning with Abraham, God no longer dealt with all of mankind. His plan was to reveal Himself and His plan through the nation of Israel, the descendants of Abraham through Isaac, and then through Jacob, Isaac's son. There is nothing "special" about Israel, the physical descendants of Abraham, except the fact that God chose them, as a nation, to be a special people.

There remains today so little understanding of what lies behind the turmoil in the Middle East. Since the re-establishment of Israel as a nation in 1948, the nations surrounding them, indeed, the world, has sought to destroy the Jewish people and Israel as a nation. Few people realize that the battle goes much deeper than a simple conflict between enemies. Just as Satan tried to stop God's plan from being fulfilled by trying to destroy the Jewish people in the days before the birth of Jesus, so he wants to stop God's plan to have Jesus return to Jerusalem and establish God's kingdom on earth. While even most of the people in Israel today or in the church do not understand these things, they are clearly revealed in the Bible.

Israel as a nation, and the Jewish people, are a "special" people to God. As we go on, we will see that this did NOT mean that all of the people of Israel would be saved; in fact, few would come to know the true God and confess their sin and worship Him. But the truth remains that God chose Israel as He chose no other nation in order to reveal Himself and His plan to send a Savior to the world. His specific promises to Abraham and his descendants will be fulfilled, just as God has said. God Himself has tied His plans to build His kingdom on earth to this people and this nation. In the eleventh chapter of his letter to the

Romans the Apostle Paul asks the question, "Did God reject His people (Israel)?" (Romans 11:1). His answer: "By no means! . . . At the present time there is a remnant chosen by grace" (Romans 11:1,5).

GRACE!! God saved Noah and his family by grace. God called Abraham to be the "father" of the nation of Israel by grace. God made His covenant with Abraham, then with Isaac and then with Jacob by grace. God made Israel a nation and chose them to be a special people unto Him by grace. None of this was deserved, none of this was earned.

And as we look further into the book of Genesis, the first book of the Bible, God continued to become more and more specific about the coming Savior. At the end of his life, Jacob gathered his sons together and blessed each of them, but to one he gave a special promise. To his son, Judah, Jacob said,

> "The scepter will not depart from Judah, nor the ruler's staff from between his feet, until he comes to whom it belongs, and the obedience of the nations is his" (Genesis 49:10).

God had said to Abraham that in his "Seed" all nations on earth would be blessed. Now He revealed that through the tribe of Judah He would bring the Savior, the One who would shed His own blood and give the perfect sacrifice for sin, and who would ultimately rule over God's people—all who would believe His promises! In the next chapter we will take a closer look at how God fulfilled His promises to Abraham, making of his descendants a great nation. We will also see how God revealed His plan of salvation, pointing ahead to the coming of the Savior, Jesus, and how He would offer Himself as a sacrifice for sin. We will see how the religion which is revealed in the Bible, true biblical Judaism, is actually the foundation of Christianity—the one and only true religion.

But in all of this, as you begin to grasp that the Bible is more than a story, that it is the unfolding of God's plan to build His kingdom on earth, remember that in spite of all the knowledge available to mankind today, knowledge which increases daily, there exists no more important knowledge that any person can have than what God reveals in His Word, the Bible. Only here can you find the truth about God, about yourself and about the way to have eternal life; only here can you discover the pathway back to God which God Himself has devised and which He reveals to His chosen people today.

Skeptics continue to mock those who claim to know the truth; others believe their religion provides them all they need to come to God. But they are all wrong!! A holy and just God cannot ignore or overlook sin—rebellion against Him. He must punish sin, and the only escape from God's judgment is faith in the Savior HE has provided: His own Son, Jesus Christ.

As you read on, ask this God to open your heart and your mind to accept these things. God has not changed since He created the world, since He created Adam and Eve. He still longs to have fellowship with His fallen creatures. The Bible says that "Faith comes from hearing the message, and the message is heard through the Word of Christ (the Messiah, the Anointed One)" (Romans 10:17).

If these things are true, then there can be only one, true religion. It is the one which God Himself revealed; the religion which knows the true God, our Creator, and which comes to Him not through some man-made ritual, but through God's own Son, the gift of God's GRACE. You CAN understand these things, as you ask God for wisdom and His Spirit becomes your Teacher. Pray now, before you go on, that God would reveal Himself to you and by His grace, give to you the gift of faith; a gift that will forever change your life; a gift that will forever change YOU!

Questions for Reflection:

God could have left mankind in our sin, being separated from Him, without any true knowledge of Him or His love and grace. But He chose to reveal Himself to His special creation and so begins His progressive plan to save those who believe in the promised Savior.

1. How does mankind's spiritual condition make GRACE absolutely necessary?

2. What characteristics of Himself does God reveal in sending the flood upon the earth in the days of Noah?

3. Why did God choose Abraham, and through him, the nation of Israel, to be His special people?

4. To whom do all of the promises made to Abraham and Israel point?

Chapter 4

"The Long Road Back!"

"A journey of a thousand miles begins with one step!" And what a journey mankind must make to return to God, to be reconciled with Him. Most people have little if any understanding of the gulf which separates each of us from eternal life in the presence of God, our Creator. In fact, it sometimes appears that those who claim to be Christians and who worship in places called churches, may have less understanding than some who follow other religions and who worship other gods. They go to church when it is convenient, and certainly want to go to heaven rather than hell (at least those who believe in hell any more), but for the most part their "faith" doesn't seem to affect the way they live. Few seem to take seriously the warnings found throughout the Bible, which they claim to believe is the very Word of God.

When asked to explain their faith, most speak in very general terms about believing in God and they may express their attempts to live a "good" life as their gift to God and as their way to get to heaven. Of course, this is NOT what the Bible teaches; nor is it the religion which the Bible reveals! Many are being deceived into believing that they are safe from God's judgment because they have a little knowledge of God in their heads, but all the while they remain separated from God by their sin because they have failed to understand the depth of their sin and the anger of God against them. They don't want to hear about hell or judgment, but only about the nice God who graciously forgives everyone, except maybe the very worst people.

Such deception is nothing new; Satan has been deceiving people with partial truth since the beginning. Satan doesn't mind if people say they believe in God, or even if they try to please God. He knows that such attempts will fail. In His "Sermon on the Mount," Jesus explained that there are two roads upon which all of mankind walks through life: a narrow road and a wide road. The narrow road is the road of "faith"; it is the road which admits our inability to find our way back to God and which follows HIS directions, relying on His grace. The wide road is the road of "works," or even "faith PLUS works"; it is the road which most people find themselves on at some point in their lives—many on their deathbeds! People who are being deceived continually think that by being good they can earn a place in heaven. Even many who claim to believe in Jesus as the promised Savior seem to think that they will ultimately get to heaven on the basis of their good works. So, they go through their religious rituals and delude themselves into thinking that all is well.

Jesus warned those who claimed to know God and to be His people to be careful, lest they be deceived. He said,

> "Enter through the narrow gate. For wide is the gate and broad is the road that leads to destruction, and many enter through it. But small is the gate and narrow the road that leads to life, and only a few find it" (Matthew 7:13–14).

Whether you will be one of the few will be determined by God's grace. Since you are reading this book, it may well be that God wants to call you as one of His own. In understanding what the Bible really teaches, you will have within your grasp the handle to the door which leads to life, the small gate which leads to the narrow road whose destination is eternal life in the presence of God! How exciting to know that God moved you to read these pages, and in reading His Word as it is quoted, and in coming to understand its message, God is calling you to put your faith in Him, to receive forgiveness for your sins, and to experience the joy of KNOWING that you have eternal life!!!

The road back to God has been a long road; a road that has crossed over centuries, as God continued to unfold His plan to gather a people who would know Him and love Him and serve Him. But a journey of a thousand miles begins with one step, and we have already seen that it was God who took the first step when He called Abraham and made His "Covenant of Grace" with him and with his descendants, the nation of Israel. Let's look more closely at how God revealed the narrow road of salvation, the road that leads to life, to Abraham and finally to the people of Israel; for as we discover the pathway to eternal life, we will find it leading us to Jesus and be moved to place our trust in Him alone.

In order to understand the Bible you MUST first understand that it records the progressive unfolding of God's plan to build His kingdom on earth. God did not reveal His whole plan at once. Step by step, over a period of some two thousand years, God prepared the world for the coming of the "Seed of the woman" promised in Genesis 3:15 and the "Seed" of Abraham promised in Genesis 12:3, through whom all the peoples on earth would be blessed. Therefore, the Bible also reveals the progressive unfolding of God's promise to bring "salvation" to mankind, to reconcile Himself with sinful creatures who had rebelled against Him and broken His law, His covenant. Like any book which records history, the Bible can only be understood when you start at the beginning and move toward the end. God does not reveal everything all at once, but He is always moving among men and ordering events to accomplish His ultimate purpose to have a people among whom He will dwell.

Remember, eternal life is knowing God and living with Him! Mankind's condition was hopeless; there was nothing any person could do to restore himself or herself to fellowship with God. But God, though just and holy, is also gracious and compassionate. Suffering and death came into the world because of mankind's rebellion against God. When people say, "Why doesn't God DO something about suffering?" what they don't understand is that God HAS done and IS doing something!! He is working through those who believe in Him to offer hope to a dying world, and He is working all things toward His desired end—a new world where those who believe will live with Him without suffering or death—FOREVER!!

To understand the long road back to God, we must understand how God, who is holy and just, can have His anger turned away from mankind; how God can forgive sin and allow those who have broken His law to live with Him. For most, this is not a problem; they believe that God has lowered His standard, that He is willing to "grade on the curve," that He will allow anyone who is sincere and who tries to please God, at least in some things and in some ways, to live with Him. Such a God does not exist in the pages of the Bible or in reality! God's standard is the same today as it was in the Garden of Eden: Perfection; nothing less will do! By ONE sin mankind became separated from God, and death, physical and spiritual death, entered the world. And each of us is now conceived and born as sinners in need of God's grace if we are to be restored into fellowship with Him.

The hope of mankind rests in GRACE—undeserved favor. Early on, God made it clear that true faith must rely on what GOD will do, and that obedience is a response to God's grace and blessing, NOT a way to EARN it!! God showed this clearly in the life of Abraham. Having blessed Abraham and Sarah with a son, Isaac, God told Abraham to take Isaac, then a young boy, the "child of promise," the one from whom God had promised to bring the "Savior"—God told Abraham to take Isaac to the top of a mountain and to offer him there as a sacrifice to God (Genesis 22).

What would YOU have done?? More than two thousand years later the writer of the book of Hebrews, inspired by God's Spirit, tells us what Abraham was thinking as he took his son, Isaac, up the mountain:

> "By faith Abraham, when God tested him, offered Isaac as a sacrifice. He who had received the promises was about to sacrifice his one and only son, even though God had said to him, 'It is through Isaac that your offspring will be reckoned.' Abraham reasoned that God could raise the dead" (Hebrews 11:17–19).

As he had done when God told him to leave his father's house and go to a place that God would show him, Abraham obeyed God. He took Isaac, and wood to build an altar, and climbed the mountain where God had commanded him to go. When Isaac asked him where the offering for the LORD was, Abraham told him, "God Himself will provide the lamb for the offering" (Genesis 22:8). Remember those words!!! GOD will provide the Lamb!! What mankind cannot do, God Himself will do. These words, spoken more than two thousand years before the birth of the Savior, the Christ, the Messiah, pointed to God's plan to save mankind through the sacrifice of His own Son, Jesus. More than two thousand years would pass as God continued to reveal Himself and to make clear the path which leads to Him! And it began here.

Abraham placed Isaac on the altar they had made together and he was about to plunge his knife into his son when the angel of the LORD called out to him and said, "Do not lay a hand on the boy . . . Now I know that you fear God, because you have not withheld from me your son, your only son" (Genesis 22:12). Then God provided a ram, caught in a thicket by its horns, for the offering, instead of Abraham's son, Isaac. So Abraham called the name of that place, "The LORD Will Provide" (Genesis 22:14).

The Bible refers often to the faith of Abraham. Many people today talk about faith as though it were some magical instrument which forces God to intervene in the lives of men. But the faith of Abraham is no mystery "force" or "inner strength"; it is the work of the very Spirit of God in the minds and hearts of His chosen people. Remember the words of the Apostle Paul,

> "By grace are you saved, through faith; and that,
> not of yourselves, it is the gift of God, not of works,
> lest any man should boast" (Ephesians 2:8–9).

True faith is always a response to God which arises out of the knowledge of God. Abraham trusted what he knew!! God had kept His promise to give Abraham and Sarah a son, though it was humanly impossible. Because Abraham knew God as faithful and trustworthy, he obeyed God without questioning Him. And the Bible says that God "credited" Abraham's faith to him as "righteousness" (Genesis 15:6). "Righteousness" is what we need to live in the presence of God. Righteousness equals "rightness," perfection in the sight of God. God's plan of salvation, revealed in the Bible, is God's way, the ONLY way, to remove our guilt and to make us holy in God's sight. FAITH is the instrument by which we receive the righteousness of God as a gift of His grace through Jesus Christ. Thus, the Apostle Paul, who had previously trusted in his own works to earn eternal life, would write,

> "I am not ashamed of the gospel, for it is the power
> of God for the salvation of everyone who believes:
> first for the Jew, then for the Gentile. For in the
> gospel a righteousness from God is revealed, a
> righteousness that is by faith" (Romans 1:16–17).

Studying Genesis and Exodus, the first two books of the Bible, is a bit like going to Kindergarten; everything you need to learn in order to understand the knowledge you will gain in the future is learned here. Skip Kindergarten and, perhaps, First Grade, and you are in trouble; yet, this is what most people do. "Righteousness" is exactly what mankind needs in order to live with God! To be "righteous" is to be "right"; it is to be good, holy, PERFECT!!! In His Sermon on the Mount, Jesus would say, "Seek first the kingdom of God and His righteousness" (Matthew 6:33). No one will stand in the presence of God without perfect righteousness! Jesus was not saying, "Try to be as good as you can so you have a chance to get to heaven." He was pointing people to accept God's offer of forgiveness through faith in Him and the sacrifice He would offer on the cross. He was pointing people to the Bible, to believe what it says about our condition and our need for God's forgiveness; our need for transformation.

As we saw in the last chapter, the problem we all face is that "there is none who is righteous; no, NOT ONE!!" But, here in Genesis, we find God talking about "crediting righteousness" to Abraham's account through the exercise of his faith in God. As we go on, we will find that such faith is a vital step on the road back to God. In reality, everyone has faith in something or someone, but it is not "true" faith—faith in the true God who keeps His promises. Some people have faith in luck, others have faith in themselves, still others have faith in some combination of man-made gods and human perseverance. None of these, however, can earn God's favor. Only a God-given faith in the God of Creation, the God who desires to reconcile Himself with His fallen creatures—only such a faith can prepare our hearts to receive God's grace, to believe that HE will provide the sacrifice which will satisfy His divine justice.

After God had prospered Abraham, then Isaac, and Isaac's son Jacob, whose name was changed to Israel because of his struggle with God, it was time to take the next step in God's plan to reveal Himself and His plan of salvation. God had made a prediction to Abraham, one that undoubtedly caused him some concern. God had told Abraham that his descendants would be strangers in a country not their own, where they would be mistreated as slaves for four hundred years (Genesis 15:13). But God had also told Abraham that He would bring his descendants back to this land and would bless them. Four hundred years is a long time. Why would God allow such a fate to befall the nation whom He had chosen to be His special people?

Throughout the Bible we find "prophecy"—predictions of the future. Some critics today claim that the passages in the Bible which predict the future were written later, after the events described had already happened. They reject the idea that anyone can know the future with such accuracy. Of course, what they really reject is a God who knows the future as He knows the past! God controls the events of mankind in such a way that He knows what choices people will make and is wise enough to use even the sinful actions of mankind to accomplish His eternal purposes.

Such was the case in the book of Exodus. The events which brought Jacob and his family down into Egypt are presented in detail in the latter chapters of Genesis. Nothing happens by chance! Some of Jacob's sons were jealous of his son, Joseph, because he was quite obviously Jacob's favorite, having been born to Rachel, the wife he loved with all his heart. Because of their jealousy, they wanted to kill Joseph, but God had other plans. Instead, they sold him as a slave and told their father he was dead. Joseph eventually ended up in Egypt and, because of his own faith in God and his patient obedience, God worked in the circumstances of his life to elevate Joseph to the throne of Egypt, where he was second in authority only to Pharaoh. In that position, he wisely prepared Egypt for a horrible famine that God was about to send on the land, and beyond, which God had revealed to Pharaoh in a dream.

When Joseph's brothers came to Egypt for food, Joseph revealed himself to them and eventually brought his father, Jacob, and his whole family to Egypt so that they would have food during the famine. As Joseph explained to his brothers, "You intended to harm me, but God intended it for good, to accomplish what is now being done, the saving of many lives" (Genesis 50:20). God used Joseph to prepare the land of Egypt for the severe famine and, because of his standing in Egypt, to save Jacob's family—the family from which the Savior would come. They were brought down into Egypt and spared from extinction!!

Now living in Egypt, God continued to bless the descendants of Jacob, and they continued to grow in number, becoming the "great nation" God had promised. But they did not forget the land of Canaan, which God had promised to Abraham's descendants. When Jacob died, they carried his body back to Canaan and he was buried in a cave that had been purchased by his grandfather, Abraham. Then, when Joseph himself was about to die, he said to his brothers and their families,

> "God will surely come to your aid and take you up out of this land to the land He promised on oath to Abraham, Isaac and Jacob" (Genesis 49:24).

Then Joseph made his brothers promise that when they returned to Canaan as a nation they would take his bones with them, so that he, too, could be buried there. Such was the faith of Joseph that he, like his forefathers, believed God's promises even when it seemed impossible that they would come to pass.

During the lifetime of Joseph and for some time afterwards, the rulers of Egypt looked with favor on the people of Israel, the descendants of Abraham, Isaac and Jacob. They lived in their own little corner of Egypt and stayed to themselves. But after nearly four hundred years the people of Israel had grown into a large nation numbering perhaps more than a million people! The Pharaoh, the ruler of Egypt, became afraid of the people of Israel, and he gave an order to have all of the male children put to death. He wanted to slow their growth and prevent them from raising an army against him. Of course, Satan was behind all of what Pharaoh was trying to do.

Yet, God would intervene once again and save a young boy named Moses. It was God's plan that Moses would lead His people out of Egypt and back to the "promised land," the land of Canaan. However, God would first use this moment in time to give a picture of the future sacrifice—which would be required to atone for mankind's sin—to point ahead to the coming of the true Deliverer, who would open the door to God's eternal kingdom, the final "Promised Land." In order to understand the Old Testament you must see God's dealings with Israel as a teaching tool which God gave to us who live after the birth, life, death, resurrection and ascension of Jesus. All that God does to deliver Israel from their slavery in Egypt is a picture of how He delivers those who believe in Jesus from their slavery to sin and brings us to live with Him. In fact, God says this very thing as He speaks through the Apostle Paul in his first letter to the church at Corinth:

> "These things happened to them as examples and were written down as warnings for us, on whom the fulfillment of the ages has come" (I Corinthians 10:11).

Through Moses God revealed His power to the Egyptians and to the people of Israel. When the Pharaoh refused to allow the people of Israel to leave Egypt to worship Him, He sent ten plagues upon the land, plagues which affected the entire land of Egypt EXCEPT where the people of Israel were living. The last of the plagues was the death of the firstborn of every household, from the Pharaoh on down. It is here that God gave another picture of how He would reconcile mankind with Himself.

God told Moses to instruct the people to take a lamb and to kill it, and then take the blood of the lamb and spread it over the doorposts of their homes. They were then to eat the rest of the lamb, along with unleavened bread, as a sign of their faith in God to provide for all their needs and to deliver them from their slavery in Egypt. Once again, faith is the instrument through which the grace of God flows to bless His people. God promised that when His angel of death saw the blood over the door, God would "pass over" that house, and the firstborn would be spared. The "blood of the lamb" pointed ahead to the sacrifice which God would provide for all who would believe, for all who would have faith.

God told Moses and the people of Israel that they were to celebrate this day as the Feast of Passover once a year to remember how God had delivered them from their slavery in Egypt. Only by God's grace were the people saved; they did nothing themselves. In the New Testament, Jesus is called our "Passover Lamb" (I Corinthians 5:7), for it is HIS blood which causes God to "pass over" our sins, to deliver us from the guilt and power of sin which enslaves us and to reconcile us to Himself. What a clear picture of the sacrifice of Jesus and the way we make that sacrifice our own—by FAITH!

After this plague, the Pharaoh finally released God's chosen people. But then he changed his mind and tried to catch them to destroy them with his army, so God opened the Red Sea so that they could cross on dry ground, and when Pharaoh and his army tried to follow, God brought the water down on top of them and they drowned. The fate of all who rebel against God is the same: destruction!! But those who trust in the LORD are saved; not only from physical destruction, but from spiritual death!! Though they had been slaves in Egypt, the worst problem the people of Israel had was their very nature; they were dead in sin. There were few who really knew God and trusted Him, as was evidenced when only a few short days after seeing the almighty power of God displayed in His destruction of Egypt and His deliverance through the Red Sea, the people began to complain because they were thirsty. Instead of trusting God to do the impossible, they complained and murmured against Him and against Moses. This would not be the last time they would do such a thing.

But it was God's desire to reveal Himself and His plan of salvation through this nation, the descendants of Abraham. And so, God brought them to Mount Sinai. The people of the nation of Israel needed to know the true God; they needed to understand His holiness and their need for a Savior. Only then would they understand the privilege of being God's chosen people and only then would they learn to rely on God's grace. So here at Mount Sinai, God gave to Israel what they needed to learn of God's holiness and of their sin: His perfect Law! The Ten Commandments!!

Later, in the book of Deuteronomy, where Moses reviews before the people the purpose of God's giving them the Law, he says, "What other nation is so great as to have such righteous decrees and laws as this body of laws I am setting before you today?" (Deuteronomy 4:8). He explains that God had shown them His wisdom and power through the plagues and their deliverance from Egypt "so that you might know that the LORD is God; besides Him there is no other!" (Deuteronomy 4:35). He says,

> "Has any other people heard the voice of God speaking out of fire, as you have, and lived? Has any god ever tried to take for himself one nation out of another nation, by testings, by miraculous signs and wonders, by war, by a mighty hand and an outstretched arm, or by great and awesome deeds?" (Deuteronomy 4:33–34).

The nations which have come against the nation of Israel in the last fifty-five years would do well to remember that the God of Israel

IS the one, true God, and that He is "jealous" for this nation like no other, even though at this time in history they have not yet accepted their Messiah, Jesus. God has promised to defend this nation and He will do what He says He will do!!

Having reminded the people of God's grace, Moses, being led by the Spirit of God, summarizes the Ten Commandments by telling the people that they are to "Love the LORD your God with all your heart and with all your soul and with all your strength" (Deuteronomy 6:5). Their obedience is to be the fruit of their faith in God; not to earn God's favor, but to thank God for His grace and the promise of a Savior who would take away their sins from before God's sight. In spite of the clear teaching of the Bible, most people fail to see that obedience is a response of love, not a boring and tedious duty to be performed out of fear. Love for God produces a willing obedience that comes from the work of God's Spirit in the hearts of those who know Him. If you are seeking to obey God or to please Him for any other reason than love, perhaps this is evidence that you do not really know Him and that you have not truly accepted His grace!

To make the picture of God's holiness and the need for a Savior even clearer, God commanded Moses and his brother, Aaron, to build a "dwelling-place" for God—a Tabernacle, where God would show Himself among the people. In the latter part of the book of Exodus, and in the book of Leviticus, we find God giving very specific instructions to Moses and the people of Israel about the way to approach God, to worship God and to have fellowship with God. Because ALL people are sinners separated from God, they need a Mediator—One who will "represent" them—who can appear before God on their behalf.

The Tabernacle was made up of two parts: the Holy Place and the Most Holy Place, or the "Holy of Holies." As we look briefly at what went on at the Tabernacle, it is important to understand that all these things were "pictures" of a reality that would take place when the Savior came. We will eventually see all of these things fulfilled perfectly in the life and ministry and sacrifice of Jesus, the Messiah, the promised Savior. We read in I Timothy 2:5, "There is one Mediator between God and men, the man Christ Jesus." And the writer of Hebrews tells us that all of these things were a shadow of things to come, for if the sacrifices offered at the Tabernacle or in the Temple which would come later could have made perfect those who were offering the sacrifices, then they would not have had to be offered over and over again (Hebrews 10:1–2). No, they were pointing to the ONE sacrifice which would be given by the Messiah, the Savior, the promised Seed of Abraham!

There were twelve "tribes" which made up the nation of Israel. As God gave the instructions for the Tabernacle, He chose the tribe of Levi to be priests. They would be the ones to offer the sacrifices which God commanded the people to offer at the Tabernacle. God chose the Levites because of their obedience to Him when the rest of the people had wanted to worship the gods of Egypt, rather than the One, True God.

The Levites, as they came to be called, represented the people before God. Outside the Tabernacle was a courtyard, where the people could enter to bring their sacrifices to God. God commanded the people to bring various sacrifices, all designed in their own way to show those who came to worship that they were "unclean" before God, but that through faith in the coming sacrifice, the one GOD Himself would provide, they could come into God's presence and have their sins forgiven and have communion with God.

When the people brought their sacrifices, the priests would offer them before the LORD and blood would be shed. God revealed that without the shedding of blood there could be no forgiveness (Leviticus 17:11). A sacrifice must be made which would satisfy God's justice. Mankind must atone for their sin before a holy God. As Adam was the representative for all of mankind, so mankind needed another representative who could reconcile them to God, their Creator.

In the sacrifices, God revealed to the people their need for this Savior over and over and over again. They were continually reminded of their sin and of God's holiness. They could not enter the Holy Place, and the priests could only enter after they had offered a sacrifice for their own sins. Then, once every year, there was a very special day. It was called the "Day of Atonement." On this day the High Priest, who at first was Aaron, the brother of Moses, could enter into the Holy of Holies.

Inside the Holy of Holies was the Ark of the Covenant. The Ark had been built at God's command and was the place where God had promised to "meet with" His people. Between the Holy Place and the Holy of Holies was a thick "curtain" which signified the separation of God from all people. On the Day of Atonement the High Priest offered sacrifices for his own sin, and went through a very strict ritual of "cleansing." He then killed a goat and took the blood behind the curtain. He sprinkled it over the cover of the Ark of the Covenant, as God had instructed, and God accepted it as a sacrifice for the sins of the people, pointing ahead to the sacrifice which the Savior would make.

After that, the High Priest took another goat and laid both of his hands on its head, confessing the sins of the people of Israel and their rebellion against God. Then he sent the goat away from the camp, into the desert, as a sign of God's forgiveness, removing the sins of the people from them. The goat was called the "scapegoat," a term used to this day to apply to one who "takes the blame" for one who is truly guilty.

Through the sacrificial system which God instituted in the time of Moses, the people of Israel could draw near to God and put their faith in the promise of God to forgive their sins through the sacrifice which He would provide. This "path" back to God was given to no other nation, to no other people on earth. Only Israel knew the true God; only Israel had a "covenant" relationship with God; only Israel had the promises of God that through the "Seed" of Abraham a Savior would come who would bring spiritual LIFE where there was only spiritual death!

Does it seem strange that God would reveal Himself in this way? Cannot God do what He wants to do? How would YOU have chosen to save sinful people?? Mankind continues to this day to refuse to accept the truth which God reveals clearly in His Word. Through the giving of His Law and in His instituting the sacrifices and ceremonies for the nation of Israel, God revealed the ONLY way to return to Him: through faith in the blood of the Lamb; through the sacrifice of One who would be our Mediator, our "Second Adam," our representative.

God reveals His plan one step at a time. In the calling of Abraham and in the establishment of the nation of Israel, God began to lay the foundation for the day in which we live today, the "day of salvation" (II Corinthians 6:2). Christianity does not begin with the birth of Jesus in a manger. Jesus is not just some "good teacher" who gives us rules to follow which might get us to heaven if we're good.

Only by understanding our sinfulness and our need for a Savior can we draw near to God.

In the coming chapters we will discover how God prepares the world for the coming of the Savior, and we will see how He keeps His promises to Abraham and his descendants, the people of Israel. Keep in mind that what we are studying and learning is intended by God to draw us to Him through faith—knowledge leading to trust and obedience. God chose Abraham and Israel not because of anything in them, but to reveal to all mankind that He alone is God and that only by grace, undeserved favor, can anyone have fellowship with Him. This is all about GOD, not us!!

The failure of mankind to recognize this truth has brought untold woe on the human race, from the time of Adam and Eve, through the flood in the days of Noah, in the foolishness of the building of the Tower of Babel and in the history of the people of Israel. When people put themselves in God's place and claim to be their own god, in control of their own lives and their own destiny, misery and destruction are sure to follow. As we trace the history of Israel we will see more and more of God's character, even as we watch a sinful human race wallow in their stubborn rebellion against their Creator.

Through the sacrifices, God pointed to the only way to be reconciled with Him, but few would find it; few would accept God's grace and love Him with all their hearts for His compassion, His patience, His kindness and His love. Few would look ahead to place their hope in God's promise to send a Savior. Like today, most only thought about their immediate "wants," and even when God met their needs, they refused to give thanks or to respond in obedience.

As we go on, we discover another picture from which we learn of future events. While God offers "salvation," while He invites people to come to Him for forgiveness and life, He shows clearly the consequences of rejecting His offer and persisting in sinful rebellion. Once again, the nation of Israel is the "illustration" of the truth which God wants you and me to understand today. As we go on, pray that you might see clearly the path which leads to LIFE and so avoid the consequences which Israel would face because of their unbelief.

Questions for Reflection:

Mankind lies spiritually dead and separated from God by sin. Only God could establish a way for His justice to be satisfied and so restore mankind to a relationship with our Creator. God Himself must provide the payment for sin and by His grace offer forgiveness to those who are unable to save themselves from His judgment.

1. What does God reveal to Abraham about the payment which must be made to satisfy His justice?

2. Explain how Abraham was "declared righteous" before God.

3. What event in the Exodus, the deliverance of the people of Israel from slavery in Egypt, pointed ahead to the sacrifice of Jesus and the shedding of His blood?

4. How did the sacrifices and ceremonies, as well as the Ten Commandments, reveal mankind's need for the Savior God had promised?

Chapter 5

"How 'Bad' Is the Human Race?"

During the latter part of the twentieth century people tried desperately to find hope amidst an ever-increasing display of depravity. Wars around the world, civil wars aimed at killing entire groups of people, crime and killing all added up to one unquestionable conclusion: the human race as a whole has a basic character flaw and we must find the solution before we destroy ourselves!!

Many sought to deny the truth and to emphasize the "good" in people. Book after book was written by those who studied human behavior, attempting to build "SELF-Esteem," thinking that if only people felt better about themselves, then they would act better, too! Of course, such thinking played right into the hands of a nature already turned toward "self"; a nature that is happy as long as it has its own way; a nature turned away from God. Many in the church bought into the philosophy that what is needed is to talk less about the law of God and the sin of man, and more about God's love and the good within each of us.

But such thinking can never lead sinful people to God and it ignores the clear teaching of God's Word that we have a desperate problem which only a complete transformation and reconciliation with God can solve. We are DEAD in sin, our spirits have no life, we are separated from God and worthy of His judgment. God offers forgiveness, "salvation," saving from His judgment which is sure to come, but we must repent; we must turn away from sin and self and come to God in humility, confessing our dependence upon Him and trusting in His grace for mercy and life. Nothing else will work to change the human heart; nothing else will bring eternal life.

Yet, most of mankind today, as they have done throughout the centuries, settles for something less—indeed, something which is but a shadow of the reality which God offers those who come to Him. Most people settle for "religion," an outward expression of devotion to God which is often guided by the ideas and traditions of men and women who claim to have a direct line of communication with God. People of all religions, including many of those who claim Christianity as their religion, want an easy way to eternal life, but what they find is a deceptive "feeling" that gives them a false sense of comfort that all is well when, in fact, they remain spiritually dead! They go through the motions of worship and add a few good deeds and may even deprive themselves of certain wants or desires, but in the end, their hearts are still turned away from God. They have invited God into their lives, but they have not turned away from the world and entered into HIS life! God says clearly in His Word that such half-hearted devotion does not reveal a heart that has been transformed by His Spirit.

> "Do not love the world or anything in the world. If anyone loves the world, the love of the Father is not in him. For everything in the world–the cravings of sinful man, the lust of his eyes and the boasting of what he has and does–comes not from the Father but from the world. The world and its desires pass away, but the man who does the will of God lives forever" (I John 2:15–17).

God and His kingdom demand FIRST place and only those who surrender to God, as His Spirit works in them, are willing to devote their lives to Him. In His Sermon on the Mount, Jesus said that on the day He returns to earth many will say to Him, "LORD, LORD, did we not prophesy in your name, and in your name drive out demons and perform many miracles?" (Matthew 7:22). But Jesus will answer, "I never knew you. Away from me, you evildoers" (Matthew 7:23).

God offers the REAL THING: a new spirit which leads to a new life! Why don't people accept what God offers? Because they don't really grasp just how bad we are; how far mankind has fallen from God; how hopeless our condition truly is!! An old song said, "There is none so blind, as he who will not see." The truth lies before us, for God has made it plain through creation, through His Word, and even in our spirits. We KNOW that we have sinned, that we have broken God's law and that we are guilty!! Yet, we choose not to confess, not to repent, not to turn to God and to accept HIS solution to our problem.

How Bad Is the Human Race?

As we look at the history of God's chosen people, Israel, we will find the record of a people who had every privilege, every advantage, every opportunity to know God and love Him and serve Him; but at every turn we will find a picture of the total depravity of the human heart—a heart turned away from God, its Creator. And we will see God's unchangeable response: disobedience brings judgment, either sooner or later!

God had revealed Himself to the whole nation of Israel through the plagues He sent upon Egypt, plagues which did not touch God's chosen people. They saw God's judgment upon sin and they saw God's grace to those who trusted in Him. God further revealed Himself in His Law, specifically, in the Ten Commandments. Moses called the people to "love the LORD with all of their heart, soul, mind and strength." Through His covenant with Abraham, God expressed His desire to enter into a relationship with mankind. We were never created to be simply "religious," to merely "practice a religion," to go through the outward rituals and traditions without any inward emotion or zeal for God. We were created for an intimate relationship with God Himself!

In the setting up of the tabernacle, as well as God's presence with Israel in a pillar of cloud by day and a pillar of fire by night as they traveled through the wilderness, God revealed His willingness to dwell with these people in a way that was different than His relationship with any other nation. Israel, and only Israel, held within their grasp the awesome promise of God that He would be their God and they would be His people. Through the sacrifices and the ceremonies which God instituted among them they were to understand their dependence upon God and their need to repent, to turn away from sin and to obey God's law. In short, as Moses stated it in Deuteronomy 30,

> "This day I call heaven and earth as witnesses against you that I have set before you life and death, blessings and curses. Now choose life, so that you and your children may live and that you may love the LORD your God, listen to His voice, and hold fast to Him. For the LORD is your Life!" (Deuteronomy 30:19–20).

So, how did Israel respond to God's call, to His invitation to enter into a relationship of love with Him? It did not take long to discover the evil that lies within the human heart, the stubborn rebellion which has taken root in the sinful mind of mankind. Reading through the books of Joshua and Judges is like taking pages from today's newspapers. Time after time after time the foolish, sinful acts of people who should have known better flash across the pages of God's Word.

Even after God had brought the nation across the Jordan river on dry ground, as He had brought them through the Red Sea when He delivered them from their slavery in Egypt; even after He had given them victory over the fortified city of Jericho, showing them that it was HIS power that would lead them into the promised land; even after God had shown Himself faithful to His promises to Abraham, Isaac and Jacob that this land would belong to them and to their descendants after them, these people still strayed away from the LORD and ignored His commands.

As the land of Canaan, now the land of Israel, was conquered and it was time for Joshua, the successor of Moses, to receive his reward, he gathered all the people together and challenged them to follow the LORD, to obey His commands and to live to worship and serve Him. The people responded, as some do today, "Far be it from us to forsake the LORD to serve other gods! . . . We, too, will serve the LORD, because He is our God" (Joshua 24:16,18). Ah, but Joshua knew all too well the nature of the human heart. He predicted what would later come to pass.

> "You are not able to serve the LORD. He is a holy God; He is a jealous God. He will not forgive your rebellion and your sins. If you forsake the LORD and serve foreign gods, He will turn and bring disaster on you, after He has been good to you" (Joshua 24:19–20).

And as we turn the pages to a short time later, into the period of the Judges, those called by God to deliver His people from the consequences of their sins, we read,

> "After that whole generation had been gathered to their fathers, another generation grew up, who

knew neither the LORD nor what He had done for Israel" (Judges 2:10).

What an incredible statement!! Had not God revealed Himself to these people time after time? Yet, they did not understand that their God was REAL, unlike the gods of the nations around them. Their hearts were hard, because their hearts were dead! The testimony of a woman named Rahab condemns the people of Israel for their ignorance, for when Joshua sent spies to the fortified city of Jericho where she lived, Rahab said to them,

> "I know that the LORD has given this land to you and that a great fear of you has fallen on us, so that all who live in this country are melting in fear because of you. We have heard how the LORD dried up the water of the Red Sea for you when you came out of Egypt, and what you did to Sihon and Og, the two kings of the Amorites east of the Jordan, whom you completely destroyed. When we heard of it, our hearts melted and everyone's courage failed because of you, for the LORD your God is God in heaven above and on the earth below" (Joshua 2:10–11).

If Rahab and the people of Jericho understood who God was, how could the people of Israel have forgotten what God had done for them? How could another generation arise who had not been told of these things—who "knew neither the LORD nor what He had done for Israel?" The answer lies in human nature, a nature dead in sin, a nature turned away from God and toward self. God had warned them of just such a thing. He had said to them through Moses,

> "When you have eaten and are satisfied, praise the LORD your God for the good land He has given you. Be careful that you do not forget the LORD your God, failing to observe His commands, His laws and His decrees. . . . Otherwise, when you eat and are satisfied, when you build fine houses and settle down, and when your herds and flocks

grow large and your silver and gold increase and all you have is multiplied, then your heart will become proud and you will forget the LORD your God, who brought you out of Egypt, out of the land of slavery" (Deuteronomy 8:10–13).

God had warned them, but human nature heeds no warnings; it is determined to go its own way. For three hundred years the people of Israel displayed the true nature of mankind. Over and over and over again they repeated the cycle of blessing, sin, judgment, repentance and deliverance. Having forgotten God, they took His blessings for granted and indulged in sinful disobedience. Then God sent their enemies against them and brought them suffering and anguish. After a time of such trials they cried out to God for deliverance and in His mercy God heard their cry and sent a "Judge" to rule over them and to help them to conquer their enemies. But as soon as they were delivered from their enemies they would return to their sinful rebellion against God, ignoring His commands and living like the people around them, and the cycle would begin all over again. Read through the book of Judges and you will find human nature at its worst. Read today's newspapers and you will have some idea of life during the time of the Judges!

Because God is gracious and compassionate, He showed His love and kindness to His people in a thousand different ways. He gave Israel their own land; He gave them victory over their enemies; He revealed Himself through His written Word, the Books of Law, the Torah, written by the hand of Moses. These people knew that they had been created in the image of God, that there was a reason for their existence as a nation and that obedience to God would bring blessing, including the promised Savior who would destroy the power of evil once and for all. They were a people who should have found their hope and their joy in God, their Deliverer!!

Instead, they treated God's blessings with the selfish, self-centered greed of a small child whose favorite word is "mine" and who is convinced that the world exists to give him or her whatever he or she wants.

If you were God, what would you have done? The God of Israel, the God of Abraham, Isaac and Jacob, IS loving, gracious and compassionate; and He is holy and just at the same time. It continued to be His unchanging purpose to reveal His own character, while at the same time revealing the character of the entire human race through the people of Israel. In His mercy, God sent the "Judges," and brought them back to Him and to His blessings. God heard the cries of His people and delivered them from their enemies and restored them to Himself.

Still, the nature within them remained unchanged. When Adam and Eve sinned against God in the Garden of Eden their spirits died; they became unable to love God with all their hearts or to obey Him fully. This nature was passed on to their offspring through the generations to follow. Though they had been created to live forever with God and to love and serve Him, they insisted on rejecting God and His plan and substituting their own plans to suit themselves and their own desires, while constantly pursuing the joy and peace and hope that only God could give them.

Though they had been chosen by God to be HIS people, they were no different than the people in the days of Noah or the Tower of Babel. As God had described mankind in those days, "that every inclination of the thoughts of his heart was only evil continually," so were these people whom God had chosen to know and love and serve Him. And finally, we read in the last verse of the book of Judges, "In those days Israel had no king; everyone did as he saw fit" (Judges 21:25).

And people say that so much has changed!! Oh, things have changed; our world is a different place today than it was even ten, twenty or thirty years ago. Those who are over sixty have seen such dramatic changes that the mind can scarcely comprehend that this is the same world. But one thing hasn't changed since the Garden of Eden; the heart of man lies spiritually dead, unable to know or love or serve God. Mankind continues in rebellion against our Creator, rejecting His Word and His truth, seeking to devise our own methods to find LIFE. We have now added the quest for the beginning of life somewhere out in space to our never-ending search for the answers to our deepest questions, answers which only God can give us. Perhaps life began on Mars or on some star far, far away!

Like the nations around Israel, mankind through the ages has manufactured its own ideas about "God" and laid out the means whereby people can feel good about themselves and their eternal destination. As Solomon, King of Israel, wrote in his book of Ecclesiastes, "God has placed eternity in the heart of man" (Ecclesiastes 3:11). People WANT to believe there is more to "life" than what we see. But all the religions of the world lead to one place: Eternal Death. Each in their own way tries to arrive at "truth," constructing a "bridge" which will lead safely to "the other side," where no man has gone, and from which no man has returned (so they think!).

To these so-called gods and man-made religions the people of Israel turned time after time. Why would they DO such a thing? Were they blind? Were they deaf? Were they ignorant? Yes! Yes!! Yes!!! Israel added to their folly by asking Samuel, the last of the Judges, to give them a king to rule over them so that they could be like the nations around them. All the other nations had a king seated on a throne. Israel had nobody to lead them—nobody, that is, but God!

Samuel was disturbed because he knew where this would lead. He wanted the people to follow God, to understand that God was their King. But they would not stop until they had a king whom they could see with their eyes. So God finally gave Israel a king to rule over them. He consoled Samuel by saying,

> "It is not you they have rejected, but they have rejected Me as their King" (I Samuel 8:7).

Such an affront to God would not go unpunished. First, He gave them the ruler they deserved, a man named Saul. He was a man who "looked like a king." He was big, strong and handsome; a "man's man." But he was a spiritual weakling. Though God gave him and Israel victories to celebrate, it was not long before he revealed his true character. He disobeyed God and ignored God's messengers and finally had the kingdom torn away from him.

Now, God would choose to teach the people something more about Himself and the Savior whom He would send—the One who would be King over God's people forever! God chose a young man named David, a young shepherd boy, to be King of Israel. And to David God gave this promise:

> "I will raise up your offspring to succeed you, . . .
> and I will establish his kingdom. He is the one
> who will build a house for my Name, and I will

establish the throne of his kingdom forever. . . . Your house and your kingdom will endure forever before me; your throne will be established forever" (II Samuel 7:12–13,16).

Do you remember God's promise to Judah, the son of Jacob? God had promised that the "scepter," the ruler's staff, would remain in the house of Judah (Genesis 49:10); that one of Judah's descendants would rule over God's people. David was a descendant of Judah, according to the plan of God. In promising that David's throne would be established forever, God was repeating the promise He had made to Judah. As time passed, God became more and more specific about His plans to bring the Savior who would save those who believed from God's judgment against their sin, so that those who came after would recognize that He was the promised One, the One anointed by God, the Messiah.

David was "a man after God's own heart" because he understood that even though he was Israel's earthly king, there was One greater than he who ruled over the heavens and the earth. God "inspired" David to write many of the songs or "Psalms" which are recorded in the Bible. These were songs which the people of Israel used in their worship and in their daily living before God. In these songs David reminded God's people who THEY were and who GOD was, so that they would turn away from their sin and seek after God.

Listen to these words of David as they accurately describe the condition of mankind:

> "The fool says in his heart, 'There is no God.' They are corrupt, their deeds are vile; there is no one who does good. The LORD looks down from heaven on the sons of men to see if there are any who understand, any who seek God. All have turned aside, they have together become corrupt; there is none who does good, not even one!"
> (Psalm 14:1–3).

And then he expresses the desire of his heart, "Oh, that salvation for Israel would come out of Zion!" (Psalm 14:7). Zion was a virtual synonym for Israel, and sometimes referred to Jerusalem, where the temple would be built, where God would meet with His people. David understood that the greatest need of God's people was to recognize God as their King and to submit to His rule. By doing so, they would experience His blessing as He dwelt among them.

Once again, God provided the opportunity for the people to experience His presence and to experience His grace. When David died, God made his son, Solomon, king over Israel. When David had desired to build a permanent "house" for God's name as a sign that He was with Israel, God had promised David that his son would be the one to build the temple. In keeping with His promise, God worked in Solomon's heart to build a "dwelling-place" for God: the temple.

Solomon's temple was a glorious picture of what lies ahead for those who come to know and love God, who live in this world by faith and trust in God's promises through Jesus Christ, His Son. Not only was it beautiful to the eye, but in the worship which God ordained to take place at the temple, He displayed once again His willingness to receive sinful man into His presence. As with the tabernacle, the sacrifices which were offered by the priests pointed to the sacrifice which God would provide when He would send the Savior.

We will look more closely at the hope which God offered to those who would believe in our next chapter, but our purpose for the moment is to fully grasp the depth of mankind's rebellion against God through the picture of the nation of Israel. In the lives of David and Solomon, men who had an intimate relationship with God, we find the same "seed" of destruction which has by now become expected, even "normal." Even these men of God exhibited the horrible consequences of their first parents, Adam and Eve.

During the reigns of David and Solomon, and all the kings who ruled after them, the kings and the people mixed the worship of God with the worship of the gods of the nations around them. Failing to understand that God is a "jealous God," who will not share His glory or honor with man-made gods, they offered God their leftover devotion and thought that by so doing they were doing God a favor!

Ignorance is NOT bliss!! To these wayward people God sent His prophets, men called and anointed by God, to speak, "Thus saith the LORD," to the people of His choosing. The prophets warned of the consequences of Israel's continued rebellion against God, and they continued to reveal the "sin problem" within man's very nature and the only means for healing. One of the greatest prophets was a man named Elijah.

Elijah lived during a time of extreme wickedness. The nation of Israel had become a divided kingdom under the reign of Solomon's son, and now the kingdom of Israel, made up of ten of the twelve tribes, and the nation of Judah, made up of the tribes of Judah and Benjamin, existed side by side, both struggling to maintain their existence among an ever-changing parade of world powers. To the eyes of the world, Israel and Judah were like any other nations: subject to the whims of rulers and armies. Some of the kings of Israel and Judah sought the true God and sought to bring revival among the people. But the revivals were never complete and were always shortened by the willful rebellion of those who should have willingly submitted to God's laws and experienced His blessing.

During the reign of one particularly wicked king whose name was Ahab, God sent the prophet Elijah to call His people to repent, to turn back to Him. After revealing God's power by calling for a drought on the land for more than three years, Elijah challenged the prophets of the false gods and testified that there was only ONE true God. He said to the people,

> "How long will you waver between two opinions?
> If the LORD is God, follow Him; but if Baal is
> God, follow Him" (I Kings 18:21).

Then, in a display of God's power, Elijah called down fire from heaven in the presence of the people and these false prophets and then called the people to return to the God of Abraham, Isaac and Jacob. The people cried out, "The LORD–He is God! The LORD–He is God" (I Kings 18:39). With their mouths, they claimed to believe. But the prophet Isaiah would declare the truth about these people when God spoke through him, saying,

> "These people come near to Me with their mouth
> and honor Me with their lips, but their hearts are
> far from Me. Their worship of Me is made up only
> of rules taught by men" (Isaiah 29:13).

The picture of man's sinful stubbornness was not yet completed.

Though the people confessed with their mouths their belief in the one, true God, their actions betrayed them, for they revealed the darkness of their hearts and the deadness of their spirits. Disobedience brings judgment, and judgment was about to come.

The northern kingdom of Israel would eventually be destroyed by the Assyrian Empire, a judgment foretold by Isaiah and other prophets sent by God to warn His people of the consequences of their idolatry. Judah would soon follow. Though God spared the nation of Judah for another one hundred fifty years, this tiny speck amidst the world powers during this period of history, these people, too, would experience the just judgment of God on a people who rejected His lordship over them.

The prophet Jeremiah predicted that they would go into exile to the nation of Babylon for seventy years. The cause? God makes it plain:

> "The heart is deceitful above all things and beyond cure. Who can understand it? I the LORD search the heart and examine the mind, to reward a man according to his conduct, according to what his deeds deserve" (Jeremiah 17:9–10).

God asks the people a question which has an obvious answer: "Can the Ethiopian change his skin or the leopard its spots? Neither can you do good who are accustomed to doing evil" (Jeremiah 13:23).

During the time when the people of Judah are in exile for their sin against their God the prophet Ezekiel would declare that they were like "dry bones," having no life in them and unable to bring life to themselves (Ezekiel 37). Over and over the prophets brought a message of impending judgment, calling the people to repent, to turn from their sin. But time and time again the people refused God's offer of forgiveness. From the first king of Israel to the destruction of the nation was but a few hundred years. But God would not forget His plan or His promises to Abraham, Isaac, Jacob and David.

If you have not yet seen the total depravity of human nature—the stubborn and foolish rebellion of people who should know better—there is still more. Even when God kept His promise and brought the Jews, the people of Judah, back from their captivity in Babylon, when He allowed them to rebuild the temple and to offer sacrifices again, when He promised to bless them if they turned to Him with all their hearts—even then these sinful, stubborn, rebellious people went their own way and rejected the God of their fathers, the God of Abraham, Isaac and Jacob, the only true God!!

All of this, from their exodus from Egypt to their return from captivity, more than a thousand years of history, to prove a point that people today still refuse to accept: Mankind is spiritually DEAD, separated from God and in need of forgiveness and life! And further, the condition of the human race is without hope, without remedy, without cure!! As Isaiah wrote in the fifty-third chapter of his book, a passage we will look at more closely in our next chapter, "We all, like sheep, have gone astray; each of us has turned to his own way" (Isaiah 53:6). Indeed, there is none, not one, who is righteous; not one who has obeyed God's law from beginning to end; not one who has loved God with his whole heart, soul, mind and strength; not one who deserves God's grace!!

Several centuries later, after Jesus had come and offered Himself as the perfect sacrifice for sin on the cross and rose again from the dead and ascended into heaven, the Apostle Paul would write about these people of Israel and explain why examining their history and learning from their mistakes is important for you and me today. Inspired, led by God's Spirit, he explained that even though the people of Israel all went through the Red Sea and experienced God's blessing as God provided for their needs through their wandering in the wilderness, yet, God was displeased with most of them.

So, Paul writes,

> "These things occurred as examples to keep us from setting our hearts on evil things as they did. . . . These things happened to them as examples and were written down as warnings for us, on whom the fulfillment of the ages has come" (I Corinthians 10:6,11).

Do you think that you and I are any different than the people of Israel or the Jews, the descendants of Abraham, Isaac and Jacob, the descendants of David?? We are not!! God's word tells us that we are all "conceived and born in sin"; we ALL like sheep have gone astray. The history of the nation of Israel is a picture of mankind's rebellion against God and of God's just judgment upon us. Sin ALWAYS brings judgment—sooner or later, sometimes both!!

As the prophets called the people to repentance in the days leading up to the birth of the Savior, so the Apostle Paul wrote after Jesus' ascension into heaven,

> "Do you think you will escape God's judgment? Or do you show contempt for the riches of His kindness, tolerance and patience, not realizing that God's kindness leads you to repentance? But because of your stubbornness and your unrepentant heart, you are storing up wrath against yourself for the day of God's wrath, when His righteous judgment will be revealed" (Romans 2:3–5).

Israel received so much from God, but gave so little. The Old Testament records the history of mankind from Adam and Eve up to about four hundred years before the birth of Jesus Christ. God revealed His holiness, His justice and His grace through Israel. He sent His prophets, His messengers, to warn them of the consequences of their sin. He showed them His willingness to forgive as He made His "dwelling-place" among them in the tabernacle and the temple. Time after time He called them to return to Him and experience His grace and His blessing.

But they would not. And so, in due time, judgment came. It was not by accident that Israel was defeated by its enemies. God predicted it through His prophets and clearly explained why it happened. These people had been called by God to display His righteousness to the world, but instead they had rejected God's rule and gone their own way.

God was not surprised. He had determined to reveal Himself through these people; and even in their rebellion God continued to reveal Himself as the only true God. In the midst of their sin, God began to reveal His plan ever more clearly to those who received His Spirit and who drew near to Him in faith. Some think that the Old Testament speaks only of sin and judgment, but nothing could be further from the truth. From the beginning, even in the Garden of Eden, God began to unfold His plan to save mankind from His just judgment against sin and so to display His love and mercy.

How Bad Is the Human Race?

In the next chapter we will look again at the history of Israel and discover another theme running through the pages of God's Word: the theme of hope!! Hope always points ahead to what "might" happen that will be good. However, the word "hope," as it is used in the Bible, goes beyond chance to the very promise of God. But before we can experience that kind of hope, hope that leads to true and eternal life—what every human being longs for—we must examine our own hearts today.

We readily brand other people as "sinners," as imperfect specimens of the human race; but most people are hesitant to label themselves as such. Like the person who refuses to admit that they are sick, people refuse to admit their true condition; they refuse to acknowledge the depth of their sin and their position before the holy God, their Creator. Refusing to confess their sin, they do not seek a cure, even as the person who refuses to admit they are sick refuses to go to the doctor. They would rather DIE first!! And they WILL!! Those who refuse to come to God for the ONLY solution for their spiritual condition will ultimately face eternal death—a fate more horrible than we can possibly imagine.

But there IS hope!! As we look more closely at the events of the people of Israel we will find that God never leaves His people without hope. No matter what your circumstances at this moment, no matter what the condition of your heart, God is speaking to you, calling you to come to Him, to acknowledge Him as the only true God and to accept Jesus as your Savior. As you read on, may you "come alive" as you experience the life-changing power of God's Word upon your heart and mind.

Questions for Reflection:

The human race has devised all sorts of religious means designed to earn God's favor. Few understand the total depravity and spiritual condition of the human heart. Yet, throughout the history of Israel, and in our own day, we see clearly the horrible consequences of sin.

1. Even after God revealed Himself clearly to the people of Israel, how does their response reveal the hardness of human hearts?

2. Describe the state of "spiritual death" which Adam and Eve experienced when they sinned against God in the Garden of Eden, and which every person born since experiences apart from the grace of God.

3. When Israel asked for a king, what were they declaring about their relationship with God?

4. Can God's just judgment ever be avoided by those who reject Him and His revelation of Himself and His plan of salvation?

Chapter 6

"HOPE - THE GIFT OF A LOVING GOD"

"Life isn't fair!" Have you ever said those words or heard someone else cry out in their anguish about the unfairness of this thing we call "life"? Problems arise, tragedies occur, things happen that are beyond our control and beyond our ability to understand. When bad things happen to people whom we consider bad people we may figure that they are getting what they deserve. But when bad things happen to people like US, to relatively good people, we begin to question the justice of the One who claims to be in control, the God of the Bible, the God of Abraham, Isaac and Jacob.

As we mentioned previously, people often ask Christians to explain the existence of evil and suffering if our God is a good and loving God as we say He is. Why don't people ever blame some of the mythological gods of the ancient Greeks or Romans? Why don't people blame their bad luck on evil spirits or demons? Why don't people try to blame their suffering on any of the gods of other religions?? Or, why don't those who claim there is no God blame themselves for their own problems?

No, when trials come nearly all people want there to be Someone to blame—so they turn to those around them who claim to believe in a God who controls all things—to Christians—and demand an answer!! "If YOUR God is in control," they ask, "then why is this happening to ME?!" Insurance policies call everything that is bad "an act of God!" Why is this so? Because within the heart of man there is the awareness that the ONLY thing that makes sense, based on the order of creation around us, is that there is a "Higher Being" who has all these things in His hands. It makes no sense to say that a storm or an "accident," or a tragedy of some kind was "an act of Luck!" Even people who don't know God or worship Him WANT to believe that there is a purpose for everything that happens.

And when you or someone else has a bad day, what do we say?? "Hang in there, tomorrow has to be better." Why? Where does this naïve sense of hope come from? Maybe things will get worse!! In fact, as we just saw in the Bible, things CAN get worse when we live in rebellion against God. The truth is: if God were "fair," you and I wouldn't even be here breathing the air and soaking up the sunshine; we would be facing His judgment at this moment. Disobedience deserves judgment; and disobedience will receive judgment—sooner or later.

Part of mankind's ignorance due to our dead spirits leaves us believing that we somehow deserve only good things. The Apostle Paul would write of the human condition and what we deserve in his letter to the Romans,

"The wages of sin is death!" (Romans 6:23).

You and I have earned death. By transgressing, by breaking God's laws, we have become debtors, guilty before a holy God. Once you sin, which means literally, "missing the mark," you cannot make it up to God. Perfection is no longer within your grasp. Your situation is hopeless. Can those who are dead bring themselves back to life? Eternal life lies beyond our grasp and eternal death awaits us. To think of such darkness overwhelms the soul, so most people make a simple choice: Don't think about it!! When confronted with the truth, people become angry and defiant and protest the injustice of their being judged. "You don't have the right to judge me!" they exclaim.

But it is God Himself that set the standard of perfection, and it is God Himself who judges the hearts and minds—and lives—of people just like you and me. Each of us must answer to GOD some day. We have already seen that God's Word says we must all stand before the judgment seat of God, and that it is appointed to each of us to die, and then to face judgment. It is an inescapable fact that no one can avoid.

Living today amidst people who brag about their sin is difficult for those who know the truth because we know that sin has consequences and we genuinely care about people—about their souls and their eternal destiny. Though some who claim to be followers of Jesus do act "superior," as though they were without sin, and sit in judgment on other people, there are others of us who know Jesus as our own personal LORD and Savior who understand and confess our own sin and are thankful for a Savior, and who therefore want to offer other people the same opportunity to confess their sin, to trust in Jesus and to receive forgiveness and eternal life. It is hard to live in this world, knowing the truth and seeing people heading toward eternal judgment, but it has always been so. The prophet Isaiah was given a vision of God on His throne in heaven, surrounded by the angels who bowed down and worshiped Him singing, "Holy, holy, holy is the LORD Almighty; the whole earth is full of His glory" (Isaiah 6:3). Isaiah's response was,

> "Woe to me! I am ruined! For I am a man of unclean lips, and I live among a people of unclean lips, and my eyes have seen the King, the LORD Almighty" (Is. 6:5).

Disaster awaits millions of unsuspecting people who have been deceived into thinking that life after death awaits them, when the truth is that eternal judgment lies just on the other side of their last breath on earth. The question of the ages does not center around why there is suffering, trials, pain and death; these come because of mankind's sin and rebellion against God. The question of the ages, rather, is this: How can sinful creatures such as you and I have ANY hope of eternal life, when we have, by our sinful thoughts, words and deeds, EARNED eternal death—eternal separation from God—eternal judgment??!! How can this holy God allow any one of us into His glorious presence?

When speaking with people who believe in a "god" other than the God who reveals Himself in His Word, the Bible, who follow their own man-made religion and who claim to have "truth," I always ask, "What do you do with your guilt??" Almost every human being knows that whatever standard might be established by a "Higher Power," you and I have failed to meet it! Virtually every religion has their set of rules, their path or road to heaven; and they all have some established means by which you can earn an afterlife, whatever that may be. Even those who believe in reincarnation believe that your position in your next life is determined by your actions in your present life.

But as we said at the beginning, there can really only be ONE true religion, and there can really only be ONE true God. Because the religions of the world contradict each other, they must ALL be wrong at some point—unless . . . unless there is one which is different and which explains, for those whose hearts and minds are open, how those who have missed the mark, who have sinned, can be forgiven, can have their hearts changed and their very natures transformed, so that they are able to enter a new world created for them by the God who created all things for His glory.

Such a religion is found in the pages of the Bible. Though it has been called "Christianity" because of the name "Christ," which means "Anointed One"—the title claimed by Jesus, the eternal Son of God, the promised Savior, when He came to earth from heaven—this one, true religion has its foundation in the One true God who reveals Himself through His Word, in the book of Genesis, as our Creator, the Creator of all things and all people. In fact, this one, true religion had its origin in the very mind of God before the world ever began. The One true God is the God who created Adam and Eve and the God who called Abraham and who gave His promises to Abraham, Isaac and Jacob. He is the God who made a great nation of Abraham's descendants, the nation of Israel, and who chose to reveal Himself and the state of mankind through this people.

HE is the God of HOPE!! Apart from Him mankind would cease to exist, and apart from Him there is no hope of eternal life. Having sinned against Him, we are all worthy of eternal judgment, and because He is a just and holy God He cannot simply overlook our sin. Atonement, payment, must be made; His justice must be satisfied. But how?? Here again is our question: How can sinful people live in the presence of God? When Adam and Eve sinned they were cast out of the Garden of Eden. They no longer had the same intimate fellowship with God which they had before.

The Bible tells us that because mankind is created in the image of God, because we are spiritual beings, we WILL live forever!! But there are two destinations: heaven or hell. You can deny the truth, but that doesn't change the truth. An old song, appropriately sung by Peter, Paul and Mary (a popular trio during the tumultuous "60's") cried out the "hope" of many then and now: "I swear there ain't no heaven, and pray there ain't no hell."

Well, by God's grace, there IS a heaven—the dwelling-place of God and His angels, but there is also a hell—the destination of all those who reject God's love and His rule over them, and who refuse to come to Him through faith in the Savior. While all the religions of the world present their "ways" to earn eternal life, the Bible says that GOD has determined THE WAY by which people, human beings, men and women, boys and girls, can be "declared righteous" by God Himself and so enter into His presence, to live with Him forever!! Jesus would say to His disciples, "I am the Way, the Truth and the Life; no one comes to the Father except through Me!"(John 14:6).

Why did He say that? HOW could He say that?? The answer lies in the Old Testament Scriptures. Let's look briefly at how God gave hope to those who understood their lost condition and how God pointed specifically to the One who would come to be the sacrifice for sin and so reconcile those who believe with God, their Creator.

God's message of hope began, appropriately enough, in the Garden of Eden. Having confronted Adam and Eve with their sin, God cursed the Serpent, Satan, and in so doing promised his defeat. God said,

> "I will put enmity between you and the woman and between your offspring and hers; He will crush your head, and you will strike His heel" (Genesis 3:15).

Some have called this the first promise of the Gospel, the good news of salvation, and indeed, it is exactly that! Having looked at the hopeless condition of mankind before a holy God in the last chapter, we should understand that there is no hope apart from God saving us; and if God must initiate our salvation, then He, and He alone, must determine what will satisfy His justice and the means by which this opportunity for forgiveness and eternal life will be offered and dispensed to mankind.

Today loud voices claim to speak for God, presenting Him as the loving God who would send no one to hell; the compassionate, merciful God who receives all people who come to Him, no matter how they come. Those who promote such tolerance on the part of God claim that the "Old Testament God" was sometimes harsh and cruel, but the "New Testament God," the One who now calls us to come to Him through His Son Jesus, is loving and kind and much more understanding of our weaknesses and sins.

The problem with such claims is that they have no foundation in the Bible. Such religion, though labeled as "Christian," is NOT biblical Christianity. The Bible presents ONE God and ONE religion. God is not one God in the centuries prior to the birth of Jesus and another God after the birth of Jesus. He is, at all times and in every age, the God of justice and holiness, AND the God of love, compassion and mercy.

Some refer to a verse in John's Gospel which says, "The law was given through Moses; grace and truth came through Jesus Christ" (John 1:17) to support their claim that there was a major shift in the dealings of God with men. It is true that the birth, life, ministry, death, resurrection and ascension of Jesus ushered in the "time of salvation," as God poured out His Spirit upon all nations (we will learn more about this later), but God's standard has never changed, for then God would necessarily have to change, and God's plan to save mankind would have to change, placing God's wisdom in question.

No, from the beginning, throughout His dealings with the people of Israel, and then Judah, God offered hope only through His grace. Centuries before Jesus was born or went to the cross, God called those who believed in Him to find their hope in the sacrifice which God Himself would provide. As the people of Israel during their time as slaves in Egypt looked for a Deliverer, so those who understood their guilt before a holy God longed for the coming of the Savior who would deliver them from the just judgment of God against their sin.

These lived by "faith," looking ahead to the fulfillment of God's promises. How many were there who understood these things? Not many. In the days of the prophet Elijah, God told him that He had reserved seven thousand who had not bowed down and worshiped the false gods of Israel and the nations around them. Seven thousand, out of several million; a "remnant," saved by the grace of God, even as He had saved Noah and his family from the flood.

Remember God's promise to Judah as his father, Jacob, blessed him,

> "The scepter will not depart from Judah, nor the ruler's staff from between his feet, until he comes to whom it belongs, and the obedience of the nations is his" (Genesis 49:10).

This was not the only evidence of God's grace in the days of Israel and Judah. Most people have heard of the story of Job. He lived some time between Abraham and David, before there was a temple. Job was a righteous man, who believed in the one, true God, the God of Abraham, Isaac and Jacob. When faced with innumerable trials and unbelievable suffering, Job declared his hope with these words,

> "I know that my Redeemer lives, and that in the end He will stand upon the earth. And after my skin has been destroyed, yet in my flesh I will see God; I myself will see Him with my own eyes" (Job 19:25–27).

At least a thousand years before Jesus is born, Job testifies that he believes in the coming Redeemer and in the forgiveness of sins and the resurrection of the dead! Though God's Spirit had not yet been poured out on mankind, some had their hearts and minds opened and received God's grace. After experiencing God's forgiveness and grace following his sin with Bathsheba, having committed adultery and murder, David returned to the LORD, confessed his sin, and proclaimed,

> "Blessed is he whose transgressions are forgiven, whose sins are covered. Blessed is the man whose sin the LORD does not count against him and in whose spirit is no deceit. . . . I acknowledged my sin to you and did not cover up my iniquity. I said, 'I will confess my transgressions to the LORD,'– and you forgave the guilt of my sin" (Psalm 32:1–2,5).

David and others who came to know God as gracious and compassionate experienced the cleansing of God's grace, even before the Savior was born. By faith they looked forward to what God would do, believing that He would keep His promise to Abraham to be a God to him and to his descendants—to all who, like Abraham, came to God in faith, believing His promises.

Again in Psalm 103 David writes,

> "Praise the LORD, O my soul; all my inmost being, praise His holy name. Praise the LORD,

> O my soul, and forget not all His benefits—who forgives all your sins and heals all your diseases, who redeems your life from the pit and crowns you with love and compassion. . . ." (vss. 1–4).

And he goes on,

> "The LORD is compassionate and gracious, slow to anger and abounding in love. He will not always accuse, nor will He harbor His anger forever; He does not treat us as our sins deserve or repay us according to our iniquities. For as high as the heavens are above the earth, so great is His love for those who fear Him; as far as the east is from the west, so far has He removed our transgressions from us" (vss. 8–12).

What beautiful words! What glorious hope!! The hope of forgiveness and the assurance of eternal life was a reality for a chosen few even in the days of the Old Testament. Some people today think it would have been so wonderful and inspiring to have lived during the Old Testament days, to see God do some of the awesome things recorded in the Bible, but they forget that during this period of history God's Spirit had not yet been sent into the world as He was after Jesus ascended into heaven. People were engulfed by spiritual darkness and only a chosen few were given the understanding to recognize God's grace in the promises of the coming Savior and to find their hope in Him. As we saw in the last chapter, this whole period of history was intended to display the horrible consequences of sin and rebellion against God which resulted in eternal death, and so to prepare the world for the Savior's birth.

Step by step God revealed His plan to send this Savior, one who would carry the burden of sin for those who believed in Him and who submitted to God's rule over them, confessing their sin and resting in God for the hope of forgiveness. Without question, the clearest expression of God's grace being offered in the coming Savior can be found in the book of the prophet Isaiah.

While many in Israel looked for a King who would deliver them from their outward enemies, Isaiah speaks of a servant, in fact, of a "suffering servant," who would accomplish the "healing" of His people. In the fifty-third chapter of his book, Isaiah reveals an unmistakable picture of the coming Savior eight hundred years before He is born.

Books have been written about this chapter of the Bible and critics have debated its authenticity. However, the discovery of the Dead Sea Scrolls has proven once again that God's Word stands firm, despite the attacks of evil men. These words were written hundreds of years before Jesus, the eternal Son of God, born of a woman, stepped foot upon the earth which He had created, and in these words we find the hope of the ages being presented in one person who, for Isaiah, was still to come at some future time. Inspired by the very mind of God, Isaiah writes as though these things had already happened, for in the mind of God it was as good as done!

> "He was despised and rejected by men, a man of sorrows and familiar with suffering.... Surely, He took up our infirmities and carried our sorrows, yet we considered Him stricken by God, smitten by Him, and afflicted. But He was pierced for our transgressions; He was crushed for our iniquities; the punishment that brought us peace was upon Him, and by His wounds we are healed" (Isaiah 53:3–5).

Does this not sound like grace to you?? Are not these words good news to hearts burdened by sin and guilt before our holy God? God had said that HE would provide the sacrifice for sin. Through Isaiah's words God describes the One who would be that sacrifice, who would take the place of sinful man before the judgment seat of God. The theological term for this judicial transaction is "substitutionary atonement." In other words, God Himself provides the substitute which will satisfy His justice. In the case of Isaac, when his father, Abraham, was about to offer him as a sacrifice to God, God provided a ram. The people of Israel were saved from the angel of death in Egypt by putting the blood of the lamb on the doorposts of their homes. The sacrifices pointed to the need for an offering to be made—a payment for sin. It is to this need that Isaiah now reveals God's provision:

> "He was pierced for OUR transgressions, He was crushed for OUR iniquities; the punishment that brought US peace was upon HIM, and by HIS wounds WE are healed" (Isaiah 53:3–5).

While the religions of the world offer their ways to God, only the Bible speaks of a transaction whereby sinful human beings have their guilt removed AND are then provided a new heart, a new mind and new LIFE within them. Not only that, but we will see that God promises those who believe a "righteousness," a perfection that will stand up to His requirements in order to live with Him. Through the Savior God will take away our sin from before His sight and "credit" to our account HIS perfect obedience, HIS perfection, as though we ourselves had obeyed God's law completely!

How many understood these words when they were first written down and read we do not know, but that they were pointing ahead to the Savior is beyond any doubt. God's grace was being offered to the people of Israel even though their darkened hearts did not understand. Isaiah goes on to say that "the LORD has laid on Him the iniquity of us all" (vs. 6). The sins of the world would be laid on this One who would be the "suffering servant" of God. His sacrifice would be enough to pay for the sins of every man, woman and child who had lived up to that time and who would live until the end of the age. In this fifty-third chapter of his book, Isaiah even described the trial of Jesus, His crucifixion between two "transgressors" and His burial in a rich man's tomb.

God had told Abraham that He would provide the sacrifice; Isaiah points ahead to the One who will BE the sacrifice for sin. And just a few verses later, in chapter fifty-five of his book, Isaiah calls people to come to God to receive His grace:

> "Seek the LORD while He may be found; call on Him while He is near. Let the wicked forsake his way and the evil man his thoughts. Let him turn to the LORD, and He will have mercy on him, and to our God, for He will freely pardon" (Isaiah 55:6–7).

God WILL have mercy on him; God WILL freely pardon.

Amazing grace!! But so few understood; so few believed and put their trust in God's promises. They lived "under the law," under the curse of God's judgment, because they were dead in sin and blinded to the grace of God. Though "children of Abraham" through the flesh, they did not receive the blessings of God's covenant with Abraham because they did not believe. The writer of the book of Hebrews would write some time after the resurrection and ascension of Jesus,

> "Since the promise of entering His (God's) rest still stands, let us be careful that none of you be found to have fallen short of it. For we also have had the gospel preached to us, just as they did; but the message they heard was of no value to them, because those who heard did not combine it with faith" (Hebrews 4:1–2).

First Israel, then Judah, faced God's judgment. The ten tribes of the northern kingdom of Israel were dispersed among the nations, but God was not through with Judah. He had promises to keep—promises of a Savior who must come from the line of David. Through the prophet Micah, God predicted that He would be born in Bethlehem (Micah 5:2). Through the prophet Zechariah, God predicted that He would enter into Jerusalem on the colt of a donkey to deliver His people (Zechariah 9:9). God gave these and other details so that when the time came, those who received His Spirit would recognize the promised One, the fulfillment of the prophecies which God made through His servants, the prophets.

The prophet Jeremiah spoke of a "new covenant" which God would make with "His people," a covenant not like the one He made with Israel through Moses, a covenant which, because of their sinful nature, they could not and did not keep. Jeremiah writes,

> "It (the new covenant) will not be like the covenant I made with their forefathers when I took them by the hand to lead them out of Egypt, because they broke My covenant. . . . This is the covenant I will make with the house of Israel after that time, . . . I will put My law in their minds and write it on their

hearts. I will be their God, and they will be My people" (Jeremiah 31:32–33).

God was predicting a time when His law would not just be an "outward" guide for people to read and try to keep; no, God would take the next step in His plan to call people out of the darkness of sin into the light of His kingdom; He would deal with the real problem of mankind since their fall into sin in the Garden of Eden, He would heal their spirits by sending His own Spirit into them, actually enabling them to see their sin, to receive His grace and to be transformed, from the inside out!

The prophet Ezekiel offered this hope to a spiritually dead people who were in captivity in Babylon when he wrote these words from the mouth of God,

"I will give you a new heart and put a new spirit in you; I will remove from you your heart of stone and give you a heart of flesh. And I will put My Spirit in you and move you to follow my decrees and be careful to keep my laws. You will live in the land I gave to your forefathers; you will be my people, and I will be your God" (Ezekiel 36:26–28).

Before His crucifixion, Jesus told His disciples that it was good for them that He was going because He would send them the Holy Spirit and the Spirit of God would teach them all things. This "new covenant" did not do away with God's law or lower His standard of righteousness, but offered hope of forgiveness and of new life by the power of God working to transform human hearts and minds. No other religion offers such a thing! No other religion offers the hope which God offered in the Old Testament Scriptures and brought to pass for those who believed.

God would build His kingdom; He would gather His people who, like Abraham, would believe in God's promises and in His Savior, the Messiah, the Anointed One, the Christ. Time after time the prophets spoke of a kingdom which would have no end. No wonder that Jesus said, "I am the Way, the Truth and the Life; no one comes to the Father except through Me!" Jesus knew that the Old Testament Scriptures pointed to Him because His Spirit moved the writers to write what they did. Yes, these things were written down for US, who are alive today!!

Millions upon millions of people all over the world today live without hope. Many, even within the Church, seem to want God to take away their earthly problems, but have little interest in eternal things or eternal life. They would be happy to live forever in this world of sin and suffering, hoping for the best. But God offers so much more!!

It was again the prophet Isaiah who first wrote of a "new heavens and a new earth." In the sixty-fifth chapter of his book he writes,

> "Behold, I will create new heavens and a new
> earth. The former things will not be remembered,
> nor will they come to mind" (Isaiah 65:17).

Thank God that He offers hope to the oppressed. Thank God that He offers grace to those who have broken His law, who have failed to keep His commands. Thank God that He keeps His promises. The writer of Hebrews would write of the gift of faith when he said,

> "Now faith is being sure of what we hope for and
> certain of what we do not see" (Hebrews 11:1).

People today hope for a lot of things that never happen, but those whose hope is in the God of grace, the God who keeps His promises, the God of Abraham, Isaac and Jacob, will not be disappointed. The Apostle Paul wrote to the believers in Rome,

> "Therefore, since we have been justified (declared righteous) through faith, we have peace with God through our LORD Jesus Christ. . . . And we rejoice in the HOPE of the glory of God. Not only so, but we also rejoice in our sufferings, because we know that suffering produces perseverance; perseverance, character; and character, HOPE. And HOPE does not disappoint us because God has poured out His love into our hearts by the Holy Spirit, whom He has given us" (Romans 5:1–5).

"Life" may not always seem fair—thank God He doesn't give us what we truly deserve. Thank God that the Scriptures of the Old

Testament pointed ahead to the One who would come to be the Savior of all who would believe. There is no hope apart from this one, true God and the Savior whom He has sent. But throughout history—HIS story—God has offered hope to those who come to Him in faith. The Bible reveals God's plan to save all who come to Him through the Savior, to give them what every human being longs for—eternal life—and to lead them even through the valley of the shadow of death, without fear, for our GOD is with us!!

Do YOU know this God? Are you living with hope every day in His promises and in His Son? God's plan was unfolding in the life of the nation of Judah; the Savior WOULD come. But not before everything was ready. We will see how God, who controls all things and all nations, prepared the world for the birth of His Son, the Savior of mankind, in order that He might fulfill His promises to Abraham and show Himself to be faithful once again. As you read, may God move you to trust Him as your God and to confess your sin and find forgiveness and life through Jesus, the Christ.

Questions for Reflection:

Even while God was revealing the total depravity of the human heart and the impossibility of mankind ever saving themselves, He offered hope through faith in the One who would take our sins upon Him and bring forgiveness and life to those who believed.

1. What question does the revelation of God's holiness and of our sinfulness lead us to ask?

2. How is the message of hope for forgiveness and eternal life which the Bible offers different than any other religion in the world?

3. As those who hoped and trusted in God during the Old Testament looked forward to the Savior God had promised, what picture does the prophet Isaiah give of this One who would come?

4. In what ways would God's "new covenant" be different than the "old covenant" He had made with Israel?

Chapter 7

"A World Without LIGHT!"

The Bible begins with these words,

> "In the beginning God created the heavens and the earth. Now the earth was formless and empty, darkness was over the surface of the deep, and the Spirit of God was hovering over the waters. And God said, 'Let there be light!'" (Genesis 1:1–3).

Imagine a world without light! But that was the physical world before God created light; a world of darkness. Darkness is symbolic of life without God, and we have seen that when mankind sinned against God, their minds and hearts were "darkened"; they could no longer see clearly or understand the things God revealed. Spiritual death—God's curse and judgment upon disobedient human beings—equals spiritual darkness. John, in his Gospel record of the life of Jesus, speaking again of the gift of the Savior, writes these words,

> "God so loved the world that He gave His one and only Son, that whoever believes in Him shall not perish but have eternal life. . . . This is the verdict: Light has come into the world, but men loved darkness instead of light because their deeds were evil" (John 3:16,19).

The tragedy of the history of the human race for the past two thousand years lies in the fact that the spiritual "light" which God shone into the world through His Son Jesus Christ, and the "light" which continues to shine through His Word, has been rejected by the bulk of mankind. LIGHT—wisdom which leads to LIFE—has shone in the darkness, but people have not grasped it; they have not understood it, because these things can be understood and accepted only when the very Spirit of God opens the mind and heart to receive them as truth. And those who do not come to this Light will spend an eternity in physical and spiritual darkness—a darkness so horrible that it cannot be adequately described by words!

God's picture of mankind through the nation of Israel was almost complete as we come to the close of the Old Testament Scriptures. The people of Israel and their kings had ignored the warnings of the prophets; they had abused the temple and the offering of sacrifices by the priests, they had turned to the gods of the nations around them, and they had failed in their calling to be the people of God. There was a "remnant" who believed, who longed for the Savior, who humbled themselves before God and pleaded for His mercy, but God's grace and His offer of salvation was rejected by most.

Surrounded by deception and lies, the people turned to those who SHOULD have led them—their religious leaders. Having been taken into captivity in Babylon, the Jews, as the people of Judah came to be called, were no longer able to worship at the temple. The "scriptures," the writings of the Old Testament, were not available for the people to read; they knew only what their teachers told them. And so these teachers became their "rabbis," the religious "experts."

While there were undoubtedly some God-fearing men among the number of the rabbis, many of them enjoyed the power and influence they had over the people and, like many teachers and religious experts today, began taking liberties with God's Word. They began to interpret God's Word for the people, to explain it in their own words rather than telling them what God Himself had said through Moses, the writer of the Torah, through the Psalms of David and others and through the prophets. Problems arose when they began to add their traditions and their man-made rules to God's unchangeable Word. Jesus would rightly condemn these religious leaders when He said,

> "You nullify the Word of God for the sake of your tradition" (Matthew 15:6).

During the four hundred years between the writing of the last prophet recorded in the Old Testament and the birth of Jesus, the religious landscape of Judah changed from being centered around the temple and the priests to being centered around the "synagogue," or meeting-place, where the rabbi taught his "students" the Torah, the book of Moses, the Law. The religion of the Jewish people had always been what gave them their identity. They were the people of God, a chosen people, the descendants of Abraham, Isaac and Jacob. As Moses had explained to them, there was nothing in them that was any better or any different than any other nation, yet God, the Creator of the universe, had chosen THEM in order to reveal Himself through His relationship with them and to reveal His plan of salvation through their worship and the words of the prophets.

Failing to understand this, most of the Jews had begun to find their identity simply in their physical relationship to Abraham. They considered themselves to be a special nation because of who THEY were, rather than because of who their GOD was. They took pride in themselves, rather than in their God. For a moment, when they returned from their captivity in Babylon, some recognized again that their identity as a special people came by grace through the God who had been faithful to His promises. The temple was rebuilt and sacrifices were again being offered which pointed ahead to the coming of the Savior.

But this moment would not last long. Very soon the religious leaders began to turn the people toward themselves and as Judah came under the rule of one world empire after another the people began to think more about the survival of their nation than about the survival of their relationship with their God. Their religion became structured around the synagogues which were established in various locations, rather than around the temple. God became a "word" or a "name" to most, while they struggled to exist in a world where they were increasingly hated. It was this "outward religion" which became known as "Judaism." The authority of the Talmud, the writings of the religious leaders, became the guide for living and their religion became like the other religions of the world—a religion of works, the means by which those who followed the prescribed path could "earn" eternal life.

While having its foundation in the Old Testament Scriptures, Judaism, as it was practiced by the populace, was virtually becoming a new religion, no longer pointing to the "Seed of the Woman," or to the descendant of Abraham, Isaac, Jacob, Judah and David, who would be King over God's people. This "new" religion did not emphasize the darkness within the human heart or the need for a Savior, and so they did not discuss God's promise to Abraham that HE would provide the sacrifice for sin.

"Judaism" became "nationalistic," in a very similar way to what threatens to happen to true biblical Christianity in this nation today. The practice of their religion, and their temple, rather than their relationship with God by faith, became for many, if not most of the Jews, their identity. While some thought of themselves as "the people of God," they did not seem to realize that they existed for God, NOT the other way around!

To be sure, the rabbis and other "sects" of religious leaders all claimed to believe in the ONE true God. They quoted the words of Moses in Deuteronomy, "The LORD our God, the LORD is one," but then they ignored God's warnings through the prophets and made up their own standard of obedience to God which grew to be a long list of "do's and don'ts." Theirs was now a religion which existed for the sake of manipulating and controlling the people, rather than a response to the grace of God, moving people to love God and to desire to please Him.

If this sounds eerily familiar to you, you can find the same thing in churches throughout our land and, perhaps, around the world today! The Bible reveals the one, true GOD, and the "practice" of the one, true religion is intended by God to be the RESPONSE of people who have come to know this one, true God; who have received His grace and who love Him and desire to serve Him as His Spirit works in their hearts. As I have stated previously, "It is not all about US, it is all about GOD!"

This one true God revealed Himself to the descendants of Abraham in order that He might in due time reveal Himself to the nations of the world. God had promised Abraham that in his "seed" ALL nations of the world would be blessed. The prophet Isaiah and others pointed to the fulfillment of God's promise. Isaiah wrote,

> "The people walking in darkness have seen a great
> light; on those living in the land of the shadow of
> death a light has dawned" (Isaiah 9:2).

According to God's plan, the descendants of Judah had to continue until the birth of this Savior, who would be King of kings! But because of their historical situation as a nation, the people wanted a

King who would do what THEY wanted—give them their own land, their own nation, and the prosperity and power that would come along with it. Judaism became, for all practical purposes, as much a political movement as a religious one. Christianity faces the same danger in our country today! Because sinful people focus on themselves and their own wants and needs, "God" comes in handy when everything else fails. If we can convince ourselves that our cause is just and that God is on our side, we will persevere through trials and suffering, continuing to believe that we will "win" in the end.

So the Jews endured through the Babylonian captivity, returning to their land and rebuilding their temple under the Persians. Though they were not truly ruling themselves, they were still hopeful that some day God would deliver them. Then came the Greeks, followed by the Romans. Various "Messiahs" came and went, claiming to be the "Deliverer" God had promised, attracting some followers, even leading revolts against those who ruled over them; but always, the outcome was the same: the Jews were slaves in their own land!

The people received from the rabbis only bits and pieces of God's Word. They knew that God had promised to restore the "throne of David," but they understood that to mean that God was going to restore the kingdom of Israel as it had been during the time of David. The prophets pointed clearly to a future "kingdom" which would have as its capital the city of Jerusalem, the city of David, and from there the coming King would rule over the nations.

What the religious leaders of the Jews did not understand was that their worst problem was not their enemies who ruled "over" them, but rather, the enemy that ruled "within" them!! God would, indeed, restore David's throne, but the "subjects" of God's kingdom must be "born again!" Those who enter God's kingdom must be brought to life by the power of God. Spiritually dead people cannot live with the one, true God.

So, the world lay in darkness, a darkness so deep, so overwhelming, that to look back over history from the perspective God gives us in His Word, there was never a time when things looked so bleak for the human race. Even the nation whom God had chosen to be His special people had spurned His love, had abused His grace and had rebelled against His law. Yes, the world lay in darkness, unable to see the light that illumines the soul, unable to find the path that leads to life! All of the religions of the world were useless, including Judaism! How frustrated God must have been!!

Oh, but God knew all this would take place. God is not surprised by the actions of mankind. He was not taken by surprise at the rebellion of Adam and Eve in the Garden; nor was He amazed at the foolish rebellion of the people of Israel. As we saw in our last chapter, disobedience always brings judgment, sooner or later. Yet, out of the sinful actions of men, God brings glory to Himself.

The history of the nation of Israel, from Jacob to Jesus, revealed two things: the character of God and the nature of man. This was God's purpose from the beginning. Through His Law God revealed His holiness and His standard of righteousness. In His dealings with Israel He revealed His patience and faithfulness, His compassion and mercy. And in His presence with His people, God revealed Himself as a personal God, unlike all the gods made up in the minds of men. As Moses asked the people in his day,

> "What other nation is so great as to have their 'gods' near them the way the LORD our God is near us whenever we pray to Him? And what other nation is so great as to have such righteous decrees and laws as this body of laws I am setting before you today?" (Deuteronomy 4:7–8).

God revealed Himself to the descendants of Abraham, the people of Israel, the Jews, in order to maintain for Himself a witness on the earth. Though most of the nation rejected His rule and no longer looked for the Messiah, the Anointed One, the One who would come as King and rule over God's people, there were a chosen few, a remnant, who "kept the faith," who maintained their hope through the centuries and who continued to stand up for the one, true God. Israel, as a nation, had a purpose in God's plan throughout the Old Testament. THEY existed for GOD!! And there were those whom God had chosen to understand these things who were still waiting for the promised One to come.

God's plan never changed. Through all of the "ups and downs" of the history of God's chosen people, God's plan never changed! The world lay in darkness as the Jewish nation languished under Roman rule. And then, one day, a day that must have seemed like any other day, an angel appeared to a young Jewish woman named Mary, and said to her,

> "Mary, you have found favor (grace) with God. You will be with child and give birth to a son, and you are to give Him the name, Jesus. He will be great and will be called the Son of the Most High. The LORD God will give Him the throne of His father, David, and He will reign over the house of Jacob forever; His kingdom will never end" (Luke 1:30–33).

Could God make His plan any clearer? His name will be "Jesus," from the Old Testament name, Joshua, which means, "The LORD saves!" He also told her that He would be the Son of the Most High. Some believe that Jesus was just a man and that He was the "son" of God in the same way that all who believe in God today are His "children." But God also sent an angel to speak to Joseph, the man engaged to be Mary's husband, telling him that the child conceived in Mary's womb was conceived by the power of God, and then, referring to the prophecy given by Isaiah (7:14) that a virgin would conceive and give birth to a child, the angel tells Joseph that this child will be "Immanuel," which means, "God with us!" This child would be a true man AND, at the same time, true God. The uniqueness of the person of Jesus reveals the uniqueness of the one, true religion which is revealed in the Bible, God's Word. God's justice required that the human nature which had sinned against Him must pay the penalty for sin. But no mere man could endure God's wrath and by so doing satisfy God's justice for himself, let alone any other person.

Therefore, this unique child would, at the same time, be true man AND true God. Paul writes to the Colossians, "In Christ all the fullness of the Deity lives in bodily form" (Colossians 2:9). Remember, these things have been written down for US!! As we continue, we will see that God's plan includes both the nation of Israel AND the Church. These are NOT two separate and exclusive attempts by God to establish His kingdom. The God of the Old Testament and the God of the New Testament are not two different "gods!" While Israel, as a nation, was, is and shall be a special nation to God, with specific promises concerning their nation and their land, God's plan from the beginning included people from every tribe, nation and language on the earth. We will find this becoming clearer and clearer as we continue through the Gospel record and into the book of Acts and the letters to the churches, which make up the New Testament.

The Apostle Paul put it this way in his letter to the Galatians,

> "When the time had fully come, God sent His Son, born of a woman, born under law, to redeem those under law (the "curse" of the law), that we might receive the full rights of sons" (Galatians 3:4–5).

As we stated at the beginning, it was God's intention to gather for Himself a people who would know Him, love Him and serve Him. Yet, people have chosen to live in the darkness rather than confess their sin—their rebellion against their Creator—and receive the "light" that only He can give, to accept the Savior HE has provided, to find forgiveness through faith in Him and to receive the gift of eternal life in God's presence.

In his Gospel record the Apostle John writes,

> "In the beginning was the Word, and the Word was with God, and the Word was God. He was with God in the beginning. Through Him all things were made; without Him nothing was made that has been made. In Him was life, and that life was the light of men. The light shines in the darkness, but the darkness has not understood it" (John 1:1–5).

The Old Testament record, the biblical record of God's dealings with mankind from creation, revealed to men by the very Spirit of God, forms the foundation for everything the New Testament teaches regarding the person and work of Jesus, the Christ, the Anointed One, the Messiah!! That the Jewish people as a nation did not recognize Jesus when He came, or accept Him as their promised King, did not surprise God. Jesus came into the world to pay the sacrifice for sin; He came into the world to be crucified on the cross of Calvary, where God would pour out His judgment upon His own Son.

While it was the Jewish leaders and others who conspired together to have Jesus crucified, it was the sin of every person who has ever lived or who ever will live that put Him on the cross. In one of the sermons which Peter preached shortly after Jesus had risen from the dead and ascended into heaven, he explained,

> "Brothers, I know that you acted in ignorance, as did your leaders. But this is how God fulfilled what He had foretold through all the prophets, saying that His Christ would suffer. Repent, then, and turn to God, so that your sins may be wiped out, that times of refreshing may come from the LORD" (Acts 3:17–19).

The religion which the New Testament reveals, what is today called "Christianity," is NOT a new religion, one which had its beginning with the birth of a man named Jesus. A true understanding of the Bible reveals that this religion which we call Christianity is the oldest religion known to man, and is, in fact, the only TRUE religion, based upon truth revealed from the mind of God, not dreamed up by the imagination of man. Perhaps we need to come up with a more accurate name for this one, true religion. Some appear to have tried to do that with the names of their churches, but few, it seems, recognize the continuity of God's plan, stretching from the beginning of the world to the end; in fact, from before creation in eternity past, to eternity future, time without end. Perhaps a better name would be "Judaic Christianity!"

Unlike all the other religions of the world, the one, true religion which is revealed in the pages of Holy Scripture is all about GOD. HE is the center, not mankind. Mankind exists for the glory of the one, true God. Several times in the pages of the Old Testament, God challenges the people of Israel to compare Him to the gods of the nations around them. In Isaiah 40, He says,

> "'To whom will you compare God?! What image will you compare Him to? . . . Do you not know? Have you not heard? Has it not been told you from the beginning? Have you not understood since the earth was founded?. . . . To whom will you

compare Me? Or who is my equal?' says the Holy One" (Isaiah 40: 18,21,25).

Yet, who was standing up for this one, true God as the world lay in darkness before the birth of Jesus? And who is standing up for this one, true God today? Religious leaders today, not only those outside of the Church, not only those who follow other religions, but those within the Church who claim to be Christian declare that there is some truth in all religions and we must be tolerant and not be judgmental. Few will stand up today and declare, "Here is truth!" God's Word reveals the ONLY way to be saved from the judgment of a holy God. And Jesus IS that way—the ONLY way to eternal life!! Perhaps we should return to the name given to the early Church by those who considered it to be a sect: "The Way" (Acts 24:14).

The failure of Israel as a nation to grasp their place in God's plan did not keep them from fulfilling God's purpose. The Savior was to come from Judah, being born in the town of Bethlehem, and so, a Roman governor named, Quirinius, governor of Syria under the Roman ruler, Caesar Augustus, became one among a long line of people who thought they were exercising their own authority when, by so doing, they became an instrument in the hands of the God who is wise enough to use even the evil of men to accomplish His purposes.

Quirinius issued a decree that all the Jews should return to the town of their forefathers in order to register for tax purposes. And since Joseph and Mary were both descendants of David, they traveled to Bethlehem, the city of David, and there, as the prophet Micah had predicted, the Savior was born!

In the words of the prophet Isaiah,

> "The people walking in darkness have seen a great light. . . . For to us a child is born, to us a son is given, and the government shall be on His shoulders. And He will be called Wonderful Counselor, Mighty God, Everlasting Father, Prince of Peace" (Isaiah 9:2,6–7)

This baby was unlike any other child ever born into this world. Some today consider the teaching of the "virgin birth" to be untrue and unnecessary, but in reality, it was absolutely necessary that the Savior be born in this miraculous way. Through the miraculous conception by the Holy Spirit in the womb of Mary, the Son of God became a man, without sin. The sinful nature of Adam was not passed on to Jesus. He was perfect in every way and as such could offer the perfect sacrifice for sin: Himself!

What so many consider to be matters only for theological debates are, in fact, the basis of our faith! Jesus was GOD in the flesh!! In his Gospel, John writes of this amazing truth,

> "The Word became flesh and made His dwelling among us. We have seen His glory, the glory of the One and Only, who came from the Father, full of grace and truth" (John 1:14).

And in his letter to the Philippians, the Apostle Paul explains further this dramatic event in human history:

> He (Jesus) "made Himself nothing, taking the very nature of a servant, being made in human likeness. And being found in appearance as a man, He humbled Himself and became obedient to death–even death on a cross" (Philippians 2:7–8).

And further, the writer of Hebrews connects the truth about WHO Jesus is, to the work He came to do:

> "The Son is the radiance of God's glory and the exact representation of His being, sustaining all things by His powerful word. After He had provided purification for sins, He sat down at the right hand of the majesty in heaven" (Hebrews 1:3).

Contrary to what many believe who have not read or studied God's Word, the Bible is NOT unclear about what is true and what is not true. God has revealed truth which becomes, for those who believe, LIGHT! The light of God's Word shines in the darkness of ignorance and gives wisdom to those who believe what God says in the Bible. So-called scholars and critics of the Bible make all kinds of claims against it in order to justify their own unbelief. It is not enough that they do not believe what it says, but they try to convince others that only a fool would put their hope in these things.

Others see the Bible and Christianity only as one of many religions which believe in "a" god. They fail again to understand the consequence of mankind's rebellion against God and the just judgment from God which comes as a result.

During His ministry Jesus proclaimed,

> "I am the light of the world! Whoever follows Me will never walk in darkness, but will have the light of life" (John 8:12).

The Pharisees, some of the religious rulers of the Jews, challenged Jesus' claim because they understood that He was claiming to be God. Others had claimed similar things but had proven themselves to be false prophets. But Jesus was different; He was, and IS, the "real thing"; He is the promised Savior, the Messiah, and the religion which Jesus taught and which we believe today is the ONLY true religion, based on the WHOLE Bible, Genesis to Revelation.

No other religion has the remedy for sin. No other religion has the formula for reconciling God with man. They all focus on what man can do to earn "God's" favor. Only the true religion, taught in the sacred writings of the prophets and apostles, revealed by the Spirit of God to the writers, confesses mankind's total dependence upon God for "salvation," for saving from His judgment which is sure to come.

No other religion understands the need for a sacrifice, a payment for sin, a payment which no sinful human being can make, in order to satisfy God's justice and thereby enable God to forgive the sins of those who believe. Anyone who reads and studies the Bible and then whose mind is opened and taught by the very Spirit of God comes to see that Jesus IS who He says He is, and that trusting in Him is the ONLY way to have eternal life.

LIGHT!! Light in the darkness! Light that is available to all men, but which most reject. Have you received the light? Have you opened your heart and mind to the truth of your sin, of God's grace and truth, and of the need for forgiveness? Have you come to Jesus Christ, the Messiah, the promised "Seed of the woman," through whom you can draw near to the God who created you, without fear of judgment?

As we go on to review the Gospel records of the life and ministry of Jesus, including His death and resurrection, and as we see the growth of the early Church and the teaching of this "new" religion, which was really the true religion fulfilled, you will see even more clearly the unfolding of God's plans and find that the basis for all that has been said thus far is firm and solid. God's Word cannot be shaken!

Questions for Reflection:

God's desire to reveal Himself takes on new meaning in the birth of Jesus, the eternal Son of God. The world lay in spiritual darkness until Jesus came as the Light of the world. Through this Light people could come to know God and receive His gracious gift of life.

1. In what did the Jews then, even as the Jews now, find their "identity" as a nation?

2. What kind of deliverance were the Jews before the birth of Jesus looking for from the Messiah?

3. Did Jesus come to establish a new religion? Explain.

4. How did the birth of Jesus bring "light" into the world?

Chapter 8

"God DID Provide!"

Unless you are blind and have learned to read with your fingers, you cannot read a book with your eyes closed; and yet, this is what many people do when it comes to the Bible. They read words, they learn lessons, they talk about stories and they treat the Bible as though it were only that—a religious book which teaches good moral lessons perhaps, but which is, after all, just a book.

The Bible remains for most people a closed book, because they do not understand the things we have seen already: that it bears the authority of God because the writers were inspired by His Spirit to write down what He wants people to know and to learn, about Him, about themselves and about His kingdom; and also, that the Bible reveals God's unchanging and unchangeable plan to reconcile those who believe in Him to Himself and to give them eternal life. The Apostle Paul rightly wrote,

> "The man without the Spirit does not accept the things that come from the Spirit of God, for they are foolishness to him; and he cannot understand them because they are spiritually discerned" (I Corinthians 2:14).

It all goes back to the condition of mankind; those whose spirits are dead will never be able to understand these things. Only the Spirit of God, the "mind of Christ" (I Corinthians 2:16) can reveal the truth of God to those who are spiritually dead. Thank God that in His grace He has chosen some to receive His Spirit and to be "born again," otherwise the entire human race would be lost and destined for eternal judgment. The confidence we have in proclaiming God's Word is that it is God's chosen instrument to bring Light and Life to some. God has promised that His Word will not "return empty, but shall accomplish what He desires and achieve the purpose for which He sent it" (Isaiah 55:11).

We began by asking if you wanted to live forever?! What we have seen as we have studied the history of the people of Israel is that, like their forefathers from Adam forward, they were sinners, worthy of God's judgment: eternal death. But we have also seen that God used the nation of Israel to reveal not only the extent of mankind's sin and separation from God, but also to reveal God's grace and His promise to provide the sacrifice for sin which would open the door to His presence and the gate to eternal life.

As we enter now into the New Testament, we need to understand why it is called the "new" testament. You may recall that the prophet Jeremiah had written that God would make a "new covenant" with His people (Jeremiah 31), and the prophet Ezekiel had also spoken of the "new" thing that God would do—that He would pour out His Spirit on His people and cause them to keep His commands (Ezekiel 36:26–27).

Throughout the time of history before the birth of Jesus Christ, the Law of God pronounced judgment upon all who broke it, and that included everybody!! Human nature was unable to keep God's law, unable to love God and unwilling to serve Him. Though God, in His grace, called a chosen few to believe in Him and gave to them His Spirit and wisdom, yet, most of mankind lay dead in sin, unable to see the light of God's glory.

But now, in the fullness of time, God sent forth His Son to redeem those who are under the curse of the law (Galatians 4:5); to set them free from their old nature of sin; to give them new hearts and to draw them to Himself by the filling of His Spirit. First, however, the sacrifice for sin, the one which all the sacrifices and ceremonies pointed to, must be given.

At first glance it becomes obvious from the Gospel record that the birth, life, death and resurrection of Jesus do not stand alone as isolated events of history. No, the Gospel record testifies from beginning to end that the ministry of Jesus stands upon the prophecies of the Old Testament Scriptures. On the opening page of Matthew's gospel, we find a genealogy of Jesus which traces His ancestry back through David, Judah, Jacob and Isaac, all the way to Abraham. The genealogy, though considered tedious reading by most, begins the testimony of God's Word concerning Jesus in order that those who read these things would immediately understand that this was a time of fulfillment. Thus is fulfilled God's promise to Abraham that in His "seed" all nations on earth would be blessed (Genesis 12:3).

And in Luke's gospel (Luke 3), the ancestry of Jesus is traced all the way back to Adam, the first man God created. Though some critics have tried to point out the "gaps" in the genealogies in order to discredit them, they stand firm as a testimony to the plan of God to save mankind from His judgment through the seed of Abraham, the descendant of David.

"Fulfillment" abounds throughout the gospels of Matthew, Mark, Luke and John. These men were all Jews, called by Jesus to be His disciples. Joseph and Mary were both Jews and so Jesus was physically and legally a Jew. Some today seem to overlook the significance of that fact, forgetting, or perhaps not even knowing that God had predicted that the Messiah would be a descendant of Judah. It has become fashionable to picture the "baby Jesus" as a child of any "color," of any "race," but if that were the case, then God is a liar and we can believe nothing of what God's Word declares to be true. The birth of Jesus marks the fulfillment of God's promises to Adam, Abraham, Isaac, Jacob, David and the whole nation of Israel! He was God in the flesh, but in His human nature Jesus was Jewish. That fact necessarily meets one of the qualifications for His being the Savior God had promised.

Even before His birth, the angels spoke to Mary and Joseph about their firstborn son. As we saw earlier, to Mary, the angel said,

> "You will be with child and give birth to a son, and you are to give him the name, Jesus. He will be great and will be called the Son of the Most High. The LORD God will give Him the throne of His father, David, and He will reign over the house of Jacob forever; His kingdom will never end" (Luke 1:31–33).

And to Joseph, the angel explains the birth of Jesus this way,

> "What is conceived in her (Mary) is from the Holy Spirit. She will give birth to a son, and you are to

give him the name Jesus, because he will save his people from their sins" (Matthew 1:21).

Then Matthew follows this with the following explanation of the events surrounding Jesus' birth:

> "All this took place to fulfill what the LORD had said through the prophet: 'The virgin will be with child and will give birth to a son, and they will call him Immanuel–which means, God with us'" (Matthew 1:22–23).

Does this sound like a "new" religion to you? Does it not rather appear to be clear that the writers of Scripture understood the birth of Jesus to be in fulfillment of God's Word?! In fact, they were not alone!! When the wise men came to worship the baby they went to the palace and asked King Herod, "Where is the one who has been born King of the Jews?" Can you imagine the look on Herod's face?! HE was King of the Jews—or, so he thought!

When the chief priest and teachers of the law were gathered together and asked where the "Christ" was to be born, they responded, "Bethlehem," and quoted the prophet Micah. They knew that the prophets predicted the coming of One who would be "anointed" by God to be ruler of Israel, the Messiah. And they knew that the prophet Micah had foretold His birthplace. It has always amazed me that they did not go with the wise men to search for the baby, but their hearts and minds were so darkened by sin that they could not accept what did not yet make sense to their minds. Few would understand these things as Jesus grew into a man and began His ministry. But as we take a few moments to examine the ministry of Jesus, remembering all that has led up to this moment of time since the Garden of Eden and mankind's fall into sin, open your mind's eyes to see these events as thousands, perhaps millions have seen them through the centuries since Jesus walked the earth—as the most exciting events ever to happen on this planet, and the most significant events for those who are searching for the secret, for the path to eternal life.

Having presented His birth as the fulfillment of the prophecies which pointed to the Messiah, the Gospel writers tell us little of the early years of Jesus' life. But the Bible tells us enough to let us know that a small remnant of the Jews had been waiting and longing for the Messiah to come. We have heard that word, "remnant," before. God saved eight people when He destroyed the earth with the flood; during the time of Elijah God told the prophet that He had reserved seven thousand souls who had not bowed the knee to the false gods; and after the captivity in Babylon, it was a "remnant" that returned to Jerusalem to rebuild the temple. As much as people today think that in order to be truly gracious God must save almost everyone, such has never been the case, nor will it be the case in the future. God IS gracious because He has decided to save many, the "remnant," when He was under no obligation to save anyone!

Two people who were part of the remnant in the days of Jesus were Simeon and Anna. Luke records the testimonies of Simeon and Anna at the temple, when Jesus' parents brought Him there to be dedicated to the LORD on the eighth day after His birth. God had revealed to Simeon that he would not die until his eyes had seen the Christ. When he took Jesus in his arms he exclaimed,

> "Sovereign LORD, as you have promised, you now dismiss your servant in peace. For my eyes have seen your salvation, which you have prepared in the sight of all people, a light for revelation to the Gentiles and for glory to your people, Israel" (Luke 2:29–32).

Anna was said to be a "prophetess" and she was eighty-four years old. As Simeon was speaking to Joseph and Mary, Anna approached them and gave thanks to God for the birth of the child and began telling everyone that the Messiah had been born. These two and others had been looking for more than a political leader; they had been waiting for the fulfillment of God's promise to send a Savior who would fulfill the sacrifices and ceremonies and make "atonement" for the sins of the people.

God also revealed the fulfillment of another prophecy from the Old Testament to Zechariah, the father of John the Baptist, whose mother Elizabeth had been unable to conceive, but who gave birth to a son just months before Jesus was born. The prophet Malachi had predicted that God would send a messenger who would prepare the way of the LORD by preparing the hearts of the people. After his son was born, Zechariah, led by the Spirit of God, predicted,

> "You, my child, will be called a prophet of the Most High; for you will go on before the LORD to prepare the way for him, to give his people the knowledge of salvation through the forgiveness of their sins" (Luke 1:76–77).

John the Baptist was used of God to prepare the people for the Gospel which would be preached after Jesus died and rose again from the dead, for he reminded the people of their sin and of their need to repent and to be saved from God's judgment. Though small in number, those who were looking for the Savior who would take away their sin would not be disappointed.

Luke also tells us of an event which took place when Jesus was but twelve years old. Having traveled to the Feast of the Passover in Jerusalem with His parents and a caravan of friends and relatives, Joseph and Mary unintentionally left without Him. When they returned to Jerusalem to find Him, He was at the temple, listening to the teachers there, asking them questions and answering theirs! When His parents asked Him why He had stayed behind, He answered, "Didn't you know I had to be in my Father's house?" (Luke 2:49).

Jesus knew who He was and what He had come to do. Some supposed biblical scholars believe that Jesus was confused as to His identity and His mission, however, it is the supposed scholars who are confused, for throughout the Gospels Jesus is found telling His disciples precisely why He had come. At one point He says, "The Son of Man came not to be served, but to serve and to give His life as a ransom for many" (Matthew 20:28, Mark 10:45). In another place He says, "The Son of Man came to seek and to save that which was lost" (Luke 19:10). Let's go forward for a moment to an event which took place sometime before His crucifixion. Jesus' ministry lasted only a few, brief years. During that time the disciples and the crowds heard Jesus preach about the kingdom of God and saw Him perform many miracles. At last Jesus asked the disciples, "Who do people say that I am?"

The disciples answered, "Some say John the Baptist (who had

been killed by this time); others say Elijah; and still others, Jeremiah or one of the prophets."

"But what about you?" Jesus asked. "Who do YOU say I am?"

Peter replied, "You are the Christ, the Son of the Living God!" (Matthew 16:13–16).

Jesus went on to tell Peter and the rest of the disciples that He would build His Church on this confession: that He was the Christ! He was the promised Messiah, the Anointed One, the Savior who would be King over God's people!! The Church, believers from every nation, would be made up of those who recognized that Jesus was the promised Messiah, the fulfillment of God's promises to Abraham. To refuse to recognize Jesus in this way is to deny the very foundation of the Church and the Gospel which the Church has been called to preach. It was NOT Peter who was the ROCK upon which the Church would be built, but his confession that Jesus was the Christ.

And they believed Him! Why? Because of the testimony of Scripture; because Jesus fulfilled every prophecy ever given about the coming "One" who would be King over God's people. Had there been anything which happened in the ministry of Jesus which contradicted what the law and prophets had foretold, it would have become obvious over time. But at every turn the life and ministry and testimony of Jesus coincided with what the Scriptures said about the One who was to come. Now, let's go back and look at some of the evidence.

As we already noted, Malachi, the last prophet of the Old Testament era, predicted that the coming King would be preceded by a Messenger; one who would come in the spirit of Elijah, preaching repentance and preparing the hearts of the people for the good news of forgiveness. John the Baptist, the cousin of Jesus who was born just a few months before Him, grew up and fulfilled this prophecy. He went about Judea preaching repentance for the forgiveness of sins. He drew a large crowd wherever he went, but when Jesus began His ministry the crowds began to follow Him.

Jesus came to John, who was baptizing people at the river, and asked John to baptize Him. John tried to avoid doing so, because God had revealed to him who Jesus was and he felt unworthy to be baptizing Jesus. But the answer Jesus gives points again to His knowledge of the purpose of His life. He said to John, "Let it be so now; it is proper for us to do this to fulfill all righteousness" (Matthew 3:15). As the

Savior, Jesus needed to fulfill every part of God's Law; He needed to be perfect, righteous, holy. He was baptized, not as a sign of repentance, for He was without sin, but as a sign of His consecration to God, His being set apart for a holy purpose, His commitment to God's calling. Though He was without sin, Jesus identified Himself with man's sin and failure and so set Himself on the path to the cross.

Immediately after Jesus was baptized, the Spirit of God descended upon Him in the form of a dove, and a voice from heaven said, "This is my Son, whom I love; with Him I am well pleased" (Matthew 3:17). God the Father had sent His Son into the world to be the perfect sacrifice for sin, to bear His judgment in our place. As heaven looked upon this incredible sight, someone else looked on, too.

After His baptism, the Gospel writers record the temptation of Jesus by Satan. As he had tempted Adam and Eve in the Garden of Eden and caused the fall of the entire human race, so now, Satan approaches the second representative of the human race. Though remarkably wise in his own right, Satan apparently believed that he could dissuade Jesus from the course God wanted Him to take, a course that would take Him to the cross to bear the horrible consequences of sin—even separation from His Father.

Satan offered Jesus an alternative, a different option. Jesus had fasted and prayed for forty days in the wilderness to prepare Himself for His ministry. Though He was God, He was also true man. His body became tired and weak. The writer of Hebrews says that He was in every way like we are, yet without sin (Hebrews 4:15). And so, Satan challenges Jesus to avoid the suffering He is enduring by commanding a stone to become bread. How does Jesus respond? He quotes the Old Testament: "It is written, 'Man does not live on bread alone, but on every word that comes from the mouth of God'" (Deuteronomy 8:3).

Next, Satan takes Jesus to the pinnacle of the temple and this time quotes Scripture himself. He says, "IF you are the Son of God, throw yourself down. For it is written, 'He will command his angels concerning you, and they will lift you up in their hands, so that you will not strike your foot against a stone'" (Psalm 91:11–12). Again, Jesus responds to Satan's distortion of God's Word by saying, "It is also written, 'Do not put the LORD your God to the test'" (Deuteronomy 6:16).

Can you imagine the nerve of Satan! Challenging Jesus, the Son of God, to a battle of Scriptures?? Finally, Satan took Jesus to a very high mountain and showed Him the kingdoms of the world. Then he offered Jesus the alternative to the cross. "All this I will give you," he said, "if you will bow down and worship me."

In effect, Satan said that he would stop fighting against God for control of the universe if Jesus would just bow down and worship him. Satan would be satisfied with this one act because he knew that in so doing, Jesus would disqualify Himself as the Savior and all mankind would be lost forever, separated from God, and God Himself would be found to be a liar, because His promised "Messiah," the one who was to defeat Satan by "crushing his head," would have failed in His mission.

But Jesus could not be outwitted by Satan. Once more He quoted Scripture, again from Deuteronomy 6, when He said, "Away from me, Satan! For it is written, 'Worship the LORD your God, and serve Him only.'"

How important for you and me to witness these things through the testimony of Scripture. The battle which had begun in heaven, the battle which had continued into the Garden of Eden, the battle between God and Satan, now took on a new dimension. As you read through the Gospel record you will find a clash between Jesus and Satan, as Jesus casts out demons and condemns the false teachers. Jesus boldly proclaims, "I am the way and the truth and the life. No one comes to the Father except through Me" (John 14:6).

The prophets had been messengers from God, but Jesus IS God! After His Sermon on the Mount, recorded in Matthew 5–7, the people were amazed at His words because "He taught as one who had authority, and not as their teachers of the law" (Matthew 7:29). Jesus made it clear that being "religious" was not the path to heaven. Though the Pharisees proclaimed the law of God and to some degree sought to be holy by keeping God's commandments, they had made their religion an outward obedience which ended up being just another "works" religion—a means by which men could earn forgiveness and a standing before God.

"Judaism" centered around "going through the motions" of offering sacrifices and celebrating the feasts and holy days. But few understood that these things pointed to the promised Savior—the

Messiah—and the sacrifice which He would offer which would atone for their sins before a holy and just God. They believed the Messiah, the Anointed One, would come as a King to destroy their enemies and to rule over Israel. So, when Jesus began talking about His death, the disciples—the twelve He had chosen to walk with Him, to learn from Him—even they didn't understand. In fact, Peter tried to talk Jesus out of it! But Jesus responded, "Get behind Me, Satan!" (Matthew 16:23).

Satan knew more about the purpose of Jesus' life than did the disciples who were closest to Him. He wanted the people to remain ignorant of God's love and of His grace; he wanted them to remain in the darkness of sin. But Jesus came to reveal God and to bring in a new era, what the New Testament writers saw as the "time of salvation" (II Corinthians 6:2). Jesus spoke about the kingdom of God and proclaimed Himself as the King. Those who had heard anything about the coming Messiah had been told that He would be King and that He would bring freedom to the captives. But we have already seen that there were also prophecies which spoke of His suffering and death. These had been ignored or explained away by the religious leaders of the Jews.

Perhaps we can understand the confusion of the people, but we cannot excuse it. The Old Testament Scriptures pointed to one who would come who would be a Prophet (Deuteronomy 18:15), a Priest (Psalm 110:4), and a King (Psalm 2:6). Many passages could be listed to support these prophecies. The prophets spoke of the restoration of Israel and of One who would be anointed by God and who would rule over the nations. We can see how the people would have been expecting one who would save them from their earthly enemies, and who would usher in an age of peace for God's chosen people.

However, as we look back at the Old Testament Scriptures, enlightened not only by history, but by the very Spirit of God, we can see what the people and the religious leaders of the Jews MISSED. They failed to understand the spiritual condition of mankind or the position of mankind before God. They failed to understand that the purpose of the Law was to convict them of their sin and to lead them to seek the Savior! They failed to understand that the purpose of the priests and the offering of the sacrifices was to show them their need for a Mediator, one to stand between them and God, and the need for a perfect sacrifice which would satisfy God's justice and take away their sin. They failed to understand that they needed to repent—to turn around, to turn away from sin—but that in order for that to happen their sinful nature needed to be overcome by the power of God. They failed to understand that it was by FAITH in God and His promises, and ultimately, by faith in the Messiah, that anyone could be reconciled to God. In short, they failed to understand God's entire plan of salvation.

They missed God's promises and the righteousness that only He could give. As he writes about his "brothers in the flesh," the Apostle Paul says,

> "I can testify that they are zealous for God, but their zeal is not based on knowledge. Since they did not know the righteousness that comes from God and sought to establish their own, they did not submit to God's righteousness" (Romans 10:2–3).

When Abraham believed God's promises all the way back in Genesis 15:6, more than two thousand years before Jesus was born, his faith was "credited to him as righteousness." It was not his own righteousness, based on his own obedience to God's law. This the Jews did not yet understand. But now, in the fullness of time, according to His plan, God sent His Son into the world to offer the sacrifice that no mere man could give. He is called by John the Baptist, "The Lamb of God who takes away the sin of the world" (John 1:29). He is the fulfillment of the Passover Lamb, whose blood spared those who believed from death (II Corinthians 5:7). The Apostle Peter writes,

> "For you know that it was not with perishable things such as silver or gold that you were redeemed from the empty way of life handed down to you from your forefathers, but with the precious blood of Christ, a lamb without blemish or defect" (I Peter 1:18–19).

THIS is what separates TRUE religion from false religion: the sacrifice of Jesus Christ, true God and true man, bearing the burden of God's wrath and judgment against sin for all who would believe in

Him. Those religious "experts" of our day who would strip the Bible of its meaning and decide for themselves which parts are true or false condemn themselves and all who would believe them. They take away the one chance anyone has of receiving the gift of eternal life through faith in Jesus, the Christ.

Jesus condemned the spiritual leaders of the Jews for their spiritual blindness. He said, "If you were blind you would not be guilty of sin; but now that you claim you can see, your guilt remains" (John 9:41). They refused to acknowledge their need for a Savior, for one who would deal with their guilt before God. They had placed their trust in a religious "system" which was intended to lead them to the Christ; but they were, indeed, blind!

At the very beginning of His ministry, Jesus had gone into the synagogue to worship and had been called upon to read the Scripture. Having been handed the scroll of the prophet, Isaiah, He read Isaiah 61:1,2:

> "The Spirit of the LORD is upon me, because He has anointed me to preach good news to the poor. He has sent me to proclaim freedom for the prisoners and recovery of sight for the blind, to release the oppressed, to proclaim the year of the LORD's favor."

Then He announced, "Today this Scripture is fulfilled in your hearing" (Luke 4:18–19). The people immediately understood that He was claiming to be the Messiah, the One anointed by the Spirit, the One Isaiah was writing about. But instead of rejoicing in God's provision, they rejected Him, even as Isaiah predicted they would (Isaiah 53), and they finally conspired against Him to crucify Him.

Jesus knew who He was AND why He had come. The war between God and Satan entered its most crucial phase. What happened here would affect the future of mankind forever. As Jesus celebrated the Passover with the disciples, the celebration which pointed to the shedding of blood to save those who believed, Jesus explained that it was HIS sacrifice, the sacrifice of HIS body and blood, which those who believed would now celebrate until He returned to earth to establish His kingdom. He told them His blood was the blood of the covenant (Mark 14:24) which God had made with Abraham, and through him, with all who believed.

Then Jesus walked with His disciples to the Garden of Gethsemane. After defeating Satan's temptations in the wilderness, Luke records that Satan "left him until an opportune time" (Luke 4:13). That time was now, just before His crucifixion. Jesus, the eternal Son of God, understood what was to come. The "price" for mankind's sin was separation from the Father. In order to pay the penalty Jesus must suffer God's wrath and judgment in the place of those He represented, those He came to save. Nothing less would do; the justice and holiness of God was at stake. And as Jesus, true God and true man, contemplates the horror of what He is about to go through, He goes to the Father in prayer to receive strength to endure what no human being has ever endured.

Satan was hard at work, seeking to stop Jesus from going to the cross. He caused the disciples to fall asleep, an act which most certainly had its affect on Jesus. Here were His closest followers, and even they did not grasp His mission or offer aid to His soul. No one has ever felt as alone as Jesus did during the time before His crucifixion and, ultimately, during the hours of darkness when He, the perfect Son of God, experienced the torment of being separated from the Father. As He prayed, alone, in the Garden of Gethsemane, He must have thought of another garden, and a choice that was made there which plunged mankind into the depths of sin. And so He prayed,

> "Father, if you are willing, take this cup from me; yet, not my will, but yours be done" (Luke 22:42).

There it is, the total surrender, the complete obedience which no man had ever given to God, but which Jesus offered in our place. He had kept the law of God perfectly, and now He offered Himself as the perfect sacrifice for sin. It was God's will that His own Son suffer for the sins you and I have committed. Amazing grace!! Isaiah had predicted as much in that 53rd chapter of his book when he wrote,

> "It was the LORD's will to crush Him and cause Him to suffer, and though the LORD makes His life a guilt offering, He will see His offspring and

prolong His days, and the will of the LORD will prosper in His hand. After the suffering of His soul, He will see the light of life and be satisfied; by His knowledge my righteous servant will justify many, and He will bear their iniquities" (Isaiah 53:10–11).

On the mountain, God had told Abraham that HE would provide the sacrifice. God had clearly said that sins could only be forgiven through the shedding of blood. The lambs which were sacrificed were a reminder of the need for such a sacrifice to be given. Now, here was Jesus, the Son of God, the perfect Lamb. God DID provide the sacrifice which satisfied His justice and brought forgiveness and life to all who would receive Jesus as their Savior and their LORD.

In His sacrifice on the cross, Jesus paid the penalty for sin and "redeemed," or purchased, those who would believe in Him to be His own. In his "Revelation," the Apostle John writes of the One who alone is worthy to open the scroll with the seven seals which begins the final countdown toward Armageddon and the return of Jesus to earth:

"You are worthy to take the scroll and to open its seals, because you were slain, and with your blood you purchased men for God from every tribe and language and people and nation" (Revelation 5:9).

After He had risen from the dead, Jesus appeared to His disciples over a period of forty days and continued to teach them. Luke records these words,

"This is what I told you while I was still with you: Everything must be fulfilled that is written about me in the Law of Moses, the Prophets and the Psalms" (Luke 24:44).

Then Luke writes that Jesus opened their minds so that they could understand the Scriptures. He didn't tell them anything "new," He didn't claim to be starting a new religion, but He opened their minds so they could understand the Old Testament Scriptures. He said to them,

> "This is what is written: The Christ will suffer and rise from the dead on the third day, and repentance and forgiveness of sins will be preached in His name to all nations, beginning at Jerusalem. You are witnesses of these things" (Luke 24:46–48).

Some might ask, "Where are these things written in the Old Testament?" The answer is, "Everywhere!" In the Torah, the books of Moses, in the Psalms and throughout the Prophets, God predicted what was to come; He pointed toward the One who would come to offer the perfect sacrifice for sin, towards which all the sacrifices pointed. Jesus taught nothing new, He simply explained the Old Testament Scriptures for all who had ears to hear—ears opened by the Spirit of God.

The promises God had made to Abraham had to be fulfilled! God cannot lie!! As we continue we will see and hear the writers of the New Testament proclaiming Jesus as the fulfillment of God's promises to Abraham. NEVER is there any mention that this is a new religion, but ALWAYS the writers refer back to the Old Testament Scriptures as their foundation for truth. In a verse we have already looked at, the Apostle Paul writes to the Galatians:

> "When the time had fully come, God sent His Son, born of a woman, born under law, to redeem those under law, that we might receive the full rights of sons" (Galatians 4:4–5).

All that the New Testament teaches is fulfillment of what God had revealed through His Word in the life of the nation of Israel. The Church today does a disservice to mankind and to the world by virtually ignoring the Old Testament and acting as though Christianity began with the birth of Jesus. The New Testament is impossible to understand without the Old Testament foundation. Yet, most people today believe that "Judaism" and "Christianity" are two separate and different religions—perhaps with common ground, but totally different in their teaching.

As we go on, we will look more closely at the Gospel, the good news of the forgiveness of sins through faith in Jesus, the Christ, at how it was proclaimed to the world, and we will see how God kept His promises to Abraham through the building of the church. It is vital that you and I understand these things, for our eternal destiny depends on our response to what God has revealed!

The spiritual blindness that plagued mankind was about to be lifted. Jesus said to His disciples shortly before His crucifixion:

> "It is for your good that I am going away. Unless I go away, the Counselor will not come to you; but if I go, I will send Him to you. . . . When He, the Spirit of truth, comes, He will guide you into all truth" (John 16:7,13).

The only cure for mankind's spiritual blindness is the Spirit of God. Jesus told Nicodemus, a Pharisee who was seeking the truth and who came to Jesus at night,

> "No one can see the kingdom of God unless he is born again . . . No one can enter the kingdom of God unless he is born of water and the Spirit" (John 3:3,5).

In the book of Acts we find the ascended LORD Jesus sending forth His Spirit into the world, fulfilling the prophecies of Ezekiel and Jeremiah and others. Under the new covenant the Spirit of God "opened the eyes" of the blind and enabled them to see Jesus as the "Seed of the woman," the "Seed of Abraham," the descendant of Judah, the "Son of David," the promised King!!

The New Testament Church thus had its beginning, but as we shall see, it did not "replace" Israel in God's plans to gather for Himself a people. Rather, it began a new "time" when God turned from one nation to the nations of the world, in fulfillment of His promise to Abraham that in his "Seed" all nations on earth would be blessed. This "new" people would be the "people of God" by faith in the Jewish Messiah, Jesus.

What plans did God have for the Church? What plans did God have for Israel? This, too, God has revealed to us in His Word. We do well to listen!

Questions for Reflection:

The New Testament can only be understood when it is recognized as the fulfillment of the Old Testament. The Jewish leaders did not see this fulfillment because of their spiritual blindness. Jesus came to fulfill God's promises to Abraham, Isaac, Jacob and Israel.

1. How did the Gospels show that the birth of Jesus was in fulfillment of Old Testament prophecies?

2. What is the importance of Jesus being recognized as the Messiah, the Christ, the Anointed One foretold in the Old Testament Scriptures?

3. What expectations did some of the Jews have for the Messiah?

4. What was mankind's greatest need and what did Jesus do to meet that need?

Chapter 9

"The Cross and the Gospel"

The climate of religious tolerance which exists today demands that everyone respect the beliefs of other people. According to the proponents of this supposed tolerance, no religion, no group of people, should claim an exclusive right to truth when it comes to spiritual things. Such claims, they say, only lead to hatred and division. The Crusades, supposedly led by "Christians," and the "Holy Wars" of Islam today are held up as examples of religious intolerance. Instead, we must all realize that religion is a sensitive subject, best left to every person to judge on his or her own what is true or false, right or wrong.

Yet, we have seen that God exhibits no such tolerance in His Word as He reveals Himself through His Son, Jesus, and as He calls people of every nation to believe in the "Jewish Messiah" in order to receive eternal life as a gift of God's grace. The Apostle Paul wrote to the believers in Corinth,

> "We preach Christ crucified: a stumbling block
> to Jews and foolishness to Gentiles, but to those
> whom God has called, both Jews and Greeks,
> Christ the power of God and the wisdom of God"
> (I Corinthians 1:23–24).

At the center of the message which Christians are called upon to proclaim to the world lies the cross upon which Jesus was crucified. What happened on the cross is what separates the one, true religion from every other religion in the world. We have already seen that it was God's plan to pour out His wrath on His own Son, Jesus—true man and true God—in order that those who believed on Him by faith would receive God's gift of forgiveness and eternal life. This truth now became the centerpiece of Christianity—the fulfillment of true, biblical Judaism.

It is important for anyone who wants to understand what the Bible teaches to consider what happened on the cross and why it remains the best news mankind has ever heard. When understood through the work of God's own Spirit within the hearts and minds of those whom He has chosen, the Gospel makes it clear that there can be no other way to have eternal life. No other religion can offer what the one true religion, presented in the Bible, offers: eternal life in the presence of God.

Certainly, the disciples and other Christians in the early Church understood this, for they committed their lives to telling others this message. There were other religions all around them. But they saw in Jesus and in the cross the only hope of forgiveness. And if you have been listening closely to God's Spirit speaking through His Word, you are beginning to understand why these things demand our attention and acceptance.

The Gospel is good news because it presents the truth that in Jesus Christ, God Himself provides the "righteousness" that every human being needs to stand in the presence of God. The prophet Isaiah had written,

> "How then can we be saved? All of us have become like one who is unclean, and all our righteous acts are like filthy rags; we all shrivel up like a leaf, and like the wind our sins sweep us away. No one calls on your name or strives to lay hold of you; for you have hidden your face from us and made us waste away because of our sins" (Isaiah 64:5–7).

Tragically, the majority of the human race has relied on offering God "filthy rags" and expecting Him to allow them into His glorious presence. Christians are called to love their neighbors as themselves, and the motivation for sharing the Gospel with those around us lies in our love for our fellow man. Christians know that those without Christ as their Mediator, their Savior from sin, are destined to face God's judgment throughout eternity in the fires of hell. When you know the destiny of those around you who do not know Jesus, love means telling them about Jesus and praying for them to accept the truth which is found only in the Bible: the Gospel—that Jesus is the Way, the Truth and the Life and that no one comes to the Father except through faith in Him.

> "For Christ's love compels us . . . because we are convinced that one died for all. . . . And He died for all, that those who live should no longer live for themselves but for Him who died for them and was raised again. . . . We are therefore Christ's ambassadors, as though God were making His appeal through us. We implore you on Christ's behalf: Be reconciled to God!" (II Corinthians 5:14–15, 20).

What is a stumbling block and foolishness to most people is the only thing which can save them from facing eternal damnation!! On the cross, and ONLY on the cross, the justice of God was satisfied and the barrier of sin which stood between God and man was removed. During the hours of darkness, as Jesus hung on the cross, God poured out His wrath on His own Son. In the midst of the darkness, Jesus cried out, "My God, my God, why have you forsaken me?" (Matthew 27:46). The judgment of Almighty God against sin is separation from Him, and in that moment on the cross the very Son of God, yet the only human being ever to keep God's law perfectly, endured hell for all who would believe in Him. And at the moment Jesus gave up His Spirit and entered into the presence of His Father, Matthew records that "the curtain of the temple was torn in two from top to bottom" (Matthew 27:51). The Most Holy Place was now open to those who would come to God through faith in His Son. Jesus had entered into the presence of the Father as our Mediator, as our great High Priest (Hebrews 4:14), and through Him all who believed now gained access to the throne of Almighty God!

No human being could make this sacrifice, for we are all guilty before God. But here on the cross is what some call "the Great Exchange." As Isaiah had predicted (Isaiah 53), God laid our sins on Him that we might be forgiven and receive the gift of life. Yes, "He was pierced for our transgressions, He was crushed for our iniquities; the punishment that brought us peace was upon Him, and by His wounds we are healed" (Isaiah 53:5).

Returning to II Corinthians 5, we find Paul continuing, "God made Him who had no sin to be sin for us, so that in Him we might become the righteousness of God" (II Corinthians 5:21). And then he goes on to say,

> "As God's fellow workers, we urge you not to receive God's grace in vain. For He says, 'In the time of favor I heard you, and in the day of salvation I helped you.' I tell you, NOW is the time of God's favor, now is the day of salvation" (II Corinthians 6:1–2).

Do away with the cross and you have done away with the Gospel. Do away with the cross and you have made Christianity like any other religion: the teachings and example of a "good" man who has long since died.

But wait, if you do away with the cross, if you deny that Jesus was who He Himself says He was, then Christianity is not even comparable to other religions; it is a total hoax. If Jesus wasn't God in the flesh, then He was a liar and a fraud and even His teaching must be discarded. If the cross of Jesus Christ did not accomplish what the New Testament writers claim it did, then Christianity is a horrible lie! You cannot have it both ways. Either Christianity is the one, true religion, going back even before time, or it is a terrible deception which gives people false hope and worse, which has cost many people their lives.

Many in the Church today are satisfied to "go to church" and worship "God" and go on about their business—concentrating on the important things in life. But these, along with the rest of the world, do not understand the danger which faces them every day. At any moment their lives on this earth could end and they would be standing before the holy God who created them and facing His judgment. In that moment they would come to understand that they were wrong, that what they failed to see is that they were not good enough to live with God forever, and that they had missed the one chance they had of escaping God's judgment by believing in His Son Jesus Christ.

Righteousness is needed to stand in the presence of God and only perfect righteousness will do. The Gospel is good news because it provides a way for those who believe in Jesus to be "credited" with

HIS righteousness in God's sight. The biblical word for this legal transaction is "Justification." Though lost amidst the centuries of darkness which fell upon the Church in the Dark Ages, the truth of "justification by faith" was rediscovered during the Reformation of the Church during the 1500's a.d.

Up to that time the Church of Rome had turned away from God's Word and had placed the authority of the Pope equal with that of the Scriptures. Ritual and tradition had replaced the Gospel of God's grace, much as ritual and tradition had replaced the way of salvation by faith in the promised Savior in the centuries before Christ's birth. Indeed, the Gospel has proven to be a stumbling block to many over the past two thousand years because mankind refuses to accept that we can do NOTHING to earn God's favor.

But once again the plan of God moved forward as men like Martin Luther and John Calvin rediscovered the truth of what had always been clear in God's Word, as the Apostle Paul had presented it to the Galatians:

> "We who are Jews by birth and not 'Gentile sinners' know that a man is not justified by observing the law, but by faith in Jesus Christ. So we, too, have put our faith in Christ Jesus that we may be justified by faith in Christ and not by observing the law, because by observing the law no one will be justified" (Galatians 3:15–16).

Paul goes on to make the connection between God's promises to Abraham and the fulfillment of the Gospel:

> "Understand, then, that those who believe are children of Abraham. The Scripture foresaw that God would justify the Gentiles by faith, and announced the Gospel in advance to Abraham: 'All nations will be blessed through you.' So those who have faith are blessed along with Abraham, the man of faith" (Galatians 3:6–9).

So few people today have ever seen this connection between what the New Testament teaches and the promises of God to Abraham more than two thousand years before Jesus was born. Many in the Church have no sense of the uniqueness of the Gospel or of the identity of believers as the "children of Abraham," and why that is important. Yet, this truth is the very foundation of "the faith" which has once for all been entrusted to the saints, the people of God today (Jude 3).

Let's look at another testimony of "justification by faith" found in Paul's letter to the Romans. First, he explains the heart of what it means to be "justified" when he says,

> "But now a righteousness FROM GOD, apart from the law, has been made known, to which the Law and the Prophets testify (not something NEW!). This righteousness from God comes through faith in Jesus Christ to all who believe. There is no difference, for all have sinned and fall short of the glory (the perfection) of God, and are justified freely by His grace through the redemption that came by Christ Jesus" (Romans 3:21–24).

And Paul even gives the reason why God did this, indeed, why this was the only way God COULD save sinful man:

> "He did it to demonstrate His justice at the present time, so as to be just and the one who justifies those who have faith in Jesus" (Romans 3:25).

We said earlier that only God could rightly determine what would satisfy His justice. His holiness demands perfection and no human being can give it!! God cannot deny His justice to satisfy His love. God cannot overlook man's sinfulness and allow him into His presence. God cannot accept the efforts of mankind to please Him by going through their religious exercises, no matter how sincere, for they do not meet HIS standard of righteousness.

Paul, a Jew, asks the question, "Is God the God of Jews only?" (Romans 3:29). He answers his own question:

> "Is He not the God of Gentiles too? Yes, of Gentiles too, since there is only one God, who will justify the circumcised by faith and the uncircumcised through the same faith" (Romans 3:29).

His conclusion, then—GOD's conclusion—is that Abraham "is the father of all who believe" (Romans 4:11). Centuries before Jesus was even born, Abraham was justified by faith; he was declared innocent by God and he was forgiven of his sins because he believed in the One who would come to provide the sacrifice which would pay the penalty for his sins. To be justified is to be declared innocent by the Judge who has the authority to make such a declaration. GOD has determined that faith in Jesus, His Son, is the ONLY way to be justified (forgiven) in His sight.

In his letter to the churches, the Apostle John shares the Gospel message this way:

> "He (Jesus) is the atoning sacrifice for our sins,
> and not only for ours but also for the sins of the
> whole world" (I John 2:2).

What Jesus accomplished on the cross was to offer to God the perfect sacrifice for sin: perfect obedience and enduring the pains of hell—separation from God. His sacrifice was sufficient for every man, woman and child who had ever lived or who ever would live. But God says there is only one way to benefit from Christ's suffering and death: Faith!

The writer of the book of Hebrews upholds the necessity of faith when he says,

> "Since the promise of entering His rest still stands,
> let us be careful that none of you be found to have
> fallen short of it. For we also have had the gospel
> preached to us, just as they did; but the message
> they heard was of no value to them, because those
> who heard did not combine it with faith" (Hebrews
> 4:1–2).

How many, even in the Church today, understand what the Bible really teaches about how to be saved from God's just judgment against our sin? How many are relying on their own religious deeds to earn them a place in heaven? How many will be surprised when in that moment when they meet God face to face, He says to them "Depart from Me, I never knew you" (Matthew 7:23).

True faith, the faith of Abraham, the faith which saves, comes to God empty-handed. We can give God absolutely NOTHING which will turn His wrath away from us. Our old natures of sin are at war with God and with His Spirit. God's Word describes the battle raging within us like this:

> "The sinful nature desires what is contrary to the Spirit, and the Spirit what is contrary to the sinful nature. They are in conflict with each other, so that you do not do what you want" (Galatians 5:17).

True faith confesses our weakness and comes to God for strength. True faith comes humbly to God, realizing that were it not for His grace we who believe in Jesus would be lost, like every person who has not put their hope in Him. True faith rejoices in God's love and mercy, because we believe, we KNOW, that through Jesus Christ we have been forgiven of ALL our sins—past, present and future—and that we are now at peace with God! Once again, we hear the word of God written by the Apostle Paul, who at one time had relied on his religious works to earn him God's favor:

> "Therefore, since we have been justified through faith, we have peace with God through our LORD Jesus Christ, through whom we have gained access by faith into this grace in which we now stand" (Romans 5:1–2).

And in perhaps the clearest explanation of the transaction which took place on the cross, Paul explains,

> "You see, at just the right time, when we were still powerless, Christ died for the ungodly. . . . God demonstrates His own love for us in this: While we were still sinners, Christ died for us. Since we have now been justified by *His blood,* how much more shall we be saved from God's wrath through Him. For if, when we were God's enemies, we were reconciled to Him through the death of His Son, how much more, having been reconciled,

shall we be saved through His life!" (Romans 5:6, 8–10).

Remember that Paul had been a Pharisee, a persecutor of Christians—until he came face to face with the risen LORD Jesus Christ on the road to Damascus. If ANYONE could claim to be religious, it would have been Paul. If today you or any other person thinks that you can stand before the true God and claim a place in His perfect presence, you need to hear what Paul wrote to the Philippians:

> "If anyone else thinks he has reasons to put confidence in the flesh, I have more: circumcised on the eighth day, of the people of Israel, of the tribe of Benjamin, a Hebrew of Hebrews; in regard to the law, a Pharisee; as for zeal, persecuting the church; as for legalistic righteousness, faultless. But whatever was to my profit I now consider loss for the sake of Christ. What is more, I consider everything a loss compared to the surpassing greatness of knowing Christ Jesus my LORD, for whose sake I have lost all things. I consider them rubbish, that I may gain Christ and be found in Him, not having a righteousness of my own that comes from the law, but that which is through faith in Christ–the righteousness that comes from God and is by faith" (Philippians 3:4–9).

How can a holy God allow sinful people into His presence? The cross and the Gospel give the only plausible answer to that question. GOD provided the sacrifice; blood was shed, the blood of the Lamb of God. "By one sacrifice He (Jesus) has made perfect forever those who are being made holy" (Hebrews 10:14). "Justification" means being declared innocent on the basis of the sacrifice which Jesus made in our place. As God sends His Holy Spirit to those whom He has chosen to belong to Him, the Spirit opens the spiritual eyes of those who were dead so that they can see God's kingdom, so that they can see that the one true God rules over all things. Then the Spirit convicts people of their sin and leads them to put their hope in Jesus, believing that He paid the price before God and so purchased our salvation—eternal life in the presence of God.

As the Spirit of God continues His work in God's chosen people, HE gives to them the gift of faith. Remember Paul's words to the Ephesian believers,

> "It is by grace you have been saved, through faith– and this, not from yourselves, it is the gift of God–not by works, so that no one can boast" (Ephesians 2:8–9).

And this one true faith, produced by the work of God's Spirit, using God's Word, results in a transformation which reveals itself in the life of every true believer. Not all who claim to be Christians really belong to God's chosen people, even as not all who were Jews were chosen to be part of God's kingdom. The horrible things done by the Christian Church during the centuries of the Dark Ages were not done by people who knew Christ, but by people who were deceived by Satan into thinking they were doing what God wanted, just as Paul thought he was pleasing God by persecuting Christians.

The work of God's Spirit produces obvious results in the lives of those who truly know and love Jesus. The "fruit" of the Spirit in the lives of true Christians, true followers of Christ Jesus, is "love, joy, peace, patience, kindness, goodness, faithfulness, gentleness and self-control" (Galatians 5:22–23). And so it is the Spirit who inspires true Christians to love others enough to tell them the truth—the truth about God, about themselves and about the only way to enter God's kingdom, to be forgiven and to receive eternal life: faith in the Jewish Messiah, the promised One, the Seed of Abraham, the Son of David, Jesus Christ, the eternal Son of God.

Religious tolerance means different things to different people. To most today it means that everyone should leave everyone else alone. Some may ask, "Why do Christians think they have to force their religion on everyone else?!" Of course, no one can or should attempt to force their religion on other people. Some Christians forget that God alone can change the hearts of those who are spiritually dead. But God has promised to use the testimony of His people to accomplish His purpose in the world. Jesus commanded His disciples to proclaim the

Gospel of forgiveness and life to the far corners of the world so that those who lived in darkness could be brought into the light!

Unlike other religions which claim to be only one path to life after death, the Bible claims that faith in Jesus is the ONLY way to eternal life. True Christians are like a doctor who knows that he has within his possession an absolute cure for cancer—the only one of its kind. Suppose people found out that such a cure has existed for years, but that the one who possessed it was keeping it to himself! The outcry would be dramatic!!

Christians are convinced, based not on the ideas or formulas of men, but on the very Word of the one true God, the Bible, that faith in Jesus is the ONLY cure for man's hopeless condition: spiritual death. We are convinced that loved ones, friends, strangers, people of all walks of life in all places of the world, stand condemned before a holy God. And it is out of love that we proclaim the truth of a righteousness that any person can receive by confessing their sin and putting their faith in Jesus Christ. To hide this cure or to deny its existence would be cruel and insensitive to those around us.

God calls His people to proclaim the good news, this Gospel of God's grace in Jesus Christ, to all people. People will often say to Christians, "Don't preach to me!" But Christians must listen to God rather than men. In His Word God says,

> "Everyone who calls on the name of the LORD will be saved. How, then, can they call on the one they have not believed in? And how can they believe in the one of whom they have not heard? And how can they hear without someone preaching to them? And how can they preach unless they are sent? As it is written, 'How beautiful are the feet of those who bring good news!'" (Romans 10:13–15).

"Tolerance" may sound nice in today's "politically correct" atmosphere, but without the Gospel, without the cross, no one will be saved from the wrath of God which will soon come upon this planet and upon all those who have not come to know Jesus, the Messiah, the Savior. For Jesus is the only Mediator between God and man, the only one who can reconcile us with God our Creator and open the door to His presence for eternity.

On that day when you stand before God, you will know that what the Bible says is true—only PERFECT righteousness will stand before God's justice. Are you perfect? Have you obeyed God perfectly? Have you kept His laws without fail? Are you "righteous?" You must either answer, "No," or declare the Bible to be a lie and everything in it false.

If, now, the Spirit of God has convicted you that you have sinned against God and that no amount of good deeds or religious conviction can ever make you righteous before God, that you are without hope of earning eternal life by your own efforts, then God calls you to come to Him through His Son Jesus Christ. Jesus said,

> "Come to me, all you who are weary and burdened, and I will give you rest. Take my yoke upon you and learn from me, for I am gentle and humble in heart, and you will find rest for your souls. For my yoke is easy and my burden is light" (Matthew 11:28–30).

Foolishly, most people think that being a Christian is a burden—that it requires depriving yourself of the fun things of life and continually feeling guilty when you do something wrong. Perhaps you know some "Christians" who live this way. But the truth is that placing your faith in Jesus is the only thing that gives life meaning and which brings freedom from guilt and fear. Knowing Jesus as your Savior means that you KNOW that you have eternal life—life forever in the presence of God in a perfect world!! And it also means that you know your sins are forgiven and that God's Spirit is working in you to produce "good fruit." You are not alone in your struggle against sin! God Himself is working in you and He will never leave you or forsake you.

To those who believe, God says, "He who began a good work in you will carry it on to completion until the day of Christ Jesus" (Philippians 1:6). Eternal life does not depend upon our efforts, but on God's grace. Therefore, the true believer can say,

> "I am convinced that neither death nor life, neither angels nor demons, neither the present nor the

> future, nor any powers, neither height nor depth, nor anything else in all creation, will be able to separate us from the love of God that is in Christ Jesus our LORD!" (Romans 8:37–39).

Does that sound like such a bad thing? The Gospel which leads us to the cross of Jesus brings to mankind exactly what every human being is searching for: eternal life!! May you be drawn to the cross by the Spirit of God even at this moment, to find in Jesus your righteousness before God, to receive forgiveness for your sins, and to find joy in serving our heavenly Father.

The way to God leads through the cross. There is no other way. But this is God's promise:

> "If we walk in the light, as He is in the light, we have fellowship with one another, and the blood of Jesus, His Son, purifies us from all sin. If we claim to be without sin, we deceive ourselves and the truth is not in us. If we confess our sins, He is faithful and just and will forgive us our sins and purify us from all unrighteousness" (I John 1:7–9).

Oh, what a glorious message! What a glorious Gospel!! No wonder that the Apostle Paul would write,

> "Even if we or an angel from heaven should preach a gospel other than the one we preached to you, let him be eternally condemned! As we have already said, so now I say again: If anybody is preaching to you a gospel other than what you accepted, let him be eternally condemned!" (Galatians 1:8–9).

Your eternal destiny depends upon your response to the Gospel which you have just heard. "Believe in the LORD Jesus Christ and you will be saved!" (Acts 16:31).

Questions for Reflection:

How can sinful people be reconciled to a Holy God? The cross stands at the center of God's plan to deliver people from His just judgment against sin and to bring them into His eternal kingdom. Through faith in Jesus those who believe receive forgiveness for their sins and the righteousness they need to enter God's presence.

1. Why is it impossible for any person to pay the penalty for their own sins and be righteous before God?

2. What does it mean to be "justified" by faith in Jesus?

3. Since those who believe are saved by grace, who receives the credit and the glory for our deliverance from sin and death?

4. How does faith in Jesus produce an assurance of eternal life that no other religion can give?

Chapter 10

"The Beginning of the Church"

Until 1948 the Church at large and most Christians in general thought very little about Israel or about the Jews as a race of people. Though some Jews had begun to return to their ancient homeland even before 1900, the events of World War II brought the plight of the Jews before the eyes of the world. Their desire to be a nation was met with hostility by their neighbors, and with indifference by the rest of the peoples of the earth. In the 1900 years before 1948, when the Jewish people WERE thought about, it was often in terms of their responsibility for crucifying Jesus and their rejection of God's Messiah. In the minds of most people who knew anything about the Bible, Israel and the Jews were no longer part of God's plan to gather a people and to build His kingdom. In the minds of many the Church had replaced Israel in God's plans. There was no more "Israel," and the Jews were no longer the "special people" of God. They were receiving the just judgment for their sins. Thus was born "anti-Semitism" toward the descendants of Noah's son, Shem, the descendants of Abraham, Isaac and Jacob.

Others, while recognizing the judgment that had fallen upon Israel, also recognized the Old Testament Scriptures which spoke about the restoration of Israel as a nation in no uncertain terms. They saw, rightly so, that these were not conditional promises, based upon Israel's obedience or disobedience, but rather, were unconditional promises which God bound Himself to keep out of His faithfulness to Abraham, Isaac and Jacob. Therefore, they studied the Scriptures of the Old and the New Testaments and saw that God had dealt with the nation of Israel to display His glory and to reveal His wisdom, His holiness and His justice, as well as His patience, mercy, compassion and grace. But further, they saw that God had revealed His plan to build His kingdom, in fulfillment of His promise to Abraham, by reaching out to ALL nations. Thus, He would build His "Church," a holy gathering of people from every tribe, nation, language and tongue.

These students of Scripture began to speak of the present age as "the Church Age," a time when God was reaching out to all the nations of the world, offering the mercy and grace which He had offered to Israel, but which had been largely rejected, except by those whose hearts God opened by His Spirit—a remnant. NOW, God would pour out His Spirit on "all flesh," and call people from all the nations—the Gentiles. As we examine the New Testament and the beginnings of the "Church," we need to answer some important questions. Who belongs to the Church? Where do the Jewish people TODAY fit into God's plan? If there is but ONE true religion, then what about Judaism? Is it a false religion? Can Jewish people be saved? How can Jews and Gentiles be brought together??

Answers to these questions appear elusive to those who are bound by their own traditions and cultures, and yet, the answers are available to all who will look to God and His Word and be led by His Spirit. In fact, the answer is quite simple: It was and is God's intent that all those whom God would choose, who would receive His Spirit and believe in His Son Jesus Christ for forgiveness and the promise of eternal life—ALL whom God would choose would be united together into ONE body: the Church!

What God has planned for Israel as a nation and the Jews as a people in the future is a separate issue which we will deal with in a moment. The important thing to understand here is that the salvation which God offered in Jesus Christ, and which He continues to offer today, was and is for ALL people, Jew and Gentile; and that all who come to God through faith in Jesus, the Jewish Messiah, will escape the judgment which will fall upon all who do not know Him and upon the whole earth. These things are clearly taught in the Bible and when rightly understood shed new light upon God's desire for the Church today and for Israel in the future.

To begin, an obvious fact which has been overlooked by most is this: the first Christians were Jews, and the beginnings of the Church were Jewish! Just as many fail to understand the importance of the Jewish ancestry of Jesus, so they fail to recognize the fact that it was Jews who were the first disciples, the first Christians and the first missionaries! Everything which we have seen up to this point has shown that Christianity is not a new religion which began with the ministry of Jesus. The one, true religion, revealed in the Bible from beginning to end, is centered around God's plan of salvation which was revealed through the Jews and which has, as its foundation, Jesus, the Jewish Messiah! According to the Bible, no other true religion exists.

While we today wonder how Jews should be brought into the Church, which is for the most part Gentile, the early Church, by God's design, was made up of Jews, and the question was how Gentiles could be brought into the "family" of God. Prior to Pentecost, fifty days after the resurrection of Jesus, the group of believers in Jerusalem had grown to about one hundred twenty people (Acts 1:15). When the Holy Spirit was sent from heaven in fulfillment of Joel's prophecy (Joel 2:28–32), we read that there were "God-fearing Jews" from every nation under heaven staying in Jerusalem for the feast. As Peter addressed the crowd which had gathered following the sound of the wind which all had heard, he said,

> "Fellow Jews and all of you who live in Jerusalem" (Acts 2:14).

It is clear that the bulk of those who received the Holy Spirit that day and who believed in Jesus Christ were Jews. They understood that Jesus was the promised Messiah who came to bring salvation to God's people. Peter quotes the prophecy of Joel and then part of Psalm 16, explaining that the words refer to Jesus' resurrection.

> "This is what was spoken by the prophet Joel: 'In the last days, God says, I will pour out my Spirit on all people. . . . And everyone who calls on the name of the LORD will be saved" (Acts 2:17–21).

> "I saw the LORD always before me. Because he is at my right hand, I will not be shaken. Therefore my heart is glad and my tongue rejoices; my body also will live in hope, because you will not abandon me to the grave, nor will you let your Holy One see decay" (Acts 2:25–27).

Then Peter also quotes David from Psalm 110 referring to one who would be his LORD. And he concludes by saying,

> "Therefore, let all Israel be assured of this: God has made this Jesus, whom you crucified, both LORD and Christ" (Acts 2:36).

"LORD and Christ!" Here again is the testimony of Peter and the disciples, all Jews, that they believed, based upon the Scriptures which they believed to be the very Word of God, that Jesus was the Christ, the promised Savior. God convicted three thousand people of their sin on the spot, and called them to repentance and faith in Jesus. In one day the Church grew from just over one hundred people, to over three thousand; and all, or at least most, were Jews! As the disciples, now apostles (ones "sent out"), continued to preach the good news of forgiveness of sins, they spoke to Jewish audiences. They continued to go to the temple at the times of prayer, but now they had a new message: God has sent the Messiah; His name is Jesus and He has risen from the dead and ascended into heaven!

In Acts 3 Peter explains these things carefully to those who had gathered after he had healed a lame man.

> "Men of Israel (Jews), why does this surprise you? . . . The God of Abraham, Isaac and Jacob, the God of our fathers, has glorified His servant Jesus . . . But this is how God fulfilled what He had foretold through all the prophets, saying that His Christ would suffer. Repent, then, and turn to God, so that your sins may be wiped out, that times of refreshing may come from the LORD, and that He may send the Christ, who has been appointed for you—even Jesus. He must remain in heaven until the time comes for God to restore everything, as He promised long ago through His holy prophets. . . . Indeed, all the prophets from Samuel on, as many as have spoken, have foretold these days. And you are heirs of the prophets and of the covenant God made with your fathers. He said to Abraham, 'Through your offspring all peoples on earth will

be blessed.' When God raised up His servant, He sent Him first to you to bless you by turning each of you from your wicked ways" (Acts 3:12–13, 18–21, 24–26).

As with the Gospels, the book of Acts contains numerous references to Old Testament Scriptures. This section of God's Word forms a bridge from the history of God's dealing nearly exclusively with the nation of Israel, to the fulfillment of His promise to Abraham that in His "Seed" ALL nations on earth would be blessed. You will notice that as Peter preaches he refers to God as the "God of Abraham, Isaac and Jacob," and that he also refers to the promise made to Abraham back in Genesis 22:18 that "Through your offspring (Seed) all peoples on earth will be blessed." At this time, even the apostles did not understand the full scope of what this meant.

While the reaction of many of the people was one of repentance and faith in Jesus, the same was not so for many of the religious leaders of the Jews. They were not convinced that Jesus was the Messiah. Their hearts were still darkened by their own sin; after all, they had been the ones who had pushed for His crucifixion, and it is always difficult to admit that we are wrong! These leaders attempted to stop what was happening by commanding the apostles not to talk about Jesus any more and by throwing them in jail. But nothing could stop the plan of God!

Peter and the others continued to preach, saying,

"We must obey God rather than men! The God of our fathers raised Jesus from the dead–whom you had killed by hanging Him on a tree. God exalted Him to His own right hand as Prince and Savior that He might give repentance and forgiveness of sins to Israel" (Acts 5:30–31).

Even in the ministry of this very early Church, it is clear that the apostles saw their mission as being primarily, if not exclusively, to the Jews. The early Church consisted almost exclusively of Jews. Therefore, what occurred was like a "civil war" among the Jews, a radical disagreement between those who accepted Jesus as the Messiah and those who didn't. What is important to truly understand is that it was not "Gentiles" who first believed in Jesus and who "broke" with "Judaism," or the Jewish religion of the day. The Gospel of Jesus Christ was first proclaimed BY Jews, TO Jews, and the early Church was made up of Jews who saw Jesus as the fulfillment of all that the prophets had said. Once again, this was NOT considered to be a new religion by those who believed in Jesus; on the contrary, it was considered to be the continuation of the oldest religion known to mankind, going back not only to Abraham, Isaac and Jacob, but through the writings of Moses in the Book of Law, the Torah, accepted by all Jews as being the inspired Word of God, all the way back to the creation of mankind, the beginning of the human race with Adam and Eve.

As Peter preached in Acts 3, he said, "When God raised up His servant, He sent Him FIRST to you" (Acts 3:26). Then, God clearly instructed the apostles to take the message of salvation to the Gentiles, according to His plan to build His kingdom from people of every tribe, nation, language and tongue. First, God spoke to a man named Saul on the road to Damascus, where he was going to persecute those who believed in Jesus. This is the man we have referred to previously who became known as Paul and who wrote many of the letters of the New Testament. Saul was a Pharisee, one of the religious leaders of the Jews, who thought that by persecuting these "Christians" they were protecting their beliefs, their religion.

However, as he was on his way, a light from heaven flashed around him and he fell to the ground. A voice from heaven spoke to him and he was struck blind. Jesus appeared to Saul and told him to go into the city and he would be told what he must do. God revealed that Saul, or Paul as he was later called by his Roman name, was God's chosen instrument to carry the Gospel before the Gentiles and their kings, AND before the people of Israel (Acts 9:15).

Though not a new religion, a new era was beginning with a new message from God Himself. The message was that the Messiah had come and God had testified to this by raising Him from the dead; therefore, all who repented (turned) from their sin and believed in Him would receive forgiveness of sins and the promise of eternal life. Nothing in the book of Acts or throughout the rest of the New Testament indicates a break in God's plan or the establishment of a new or different religion.

God now revealed to Peter in a vision that the message of salvation should also be preached to the Gentiles, those who were not of Jewish descent. Acts 10 records Peter's reaction when told to take the Gospel to the Gentiles, but he could not argue with God! In fact, he responds,

> "I now realize how true it is that God does not show favoritism but accepts men from every nation who fear Him and do what is right" (Acts 10:35).

Peter then proclaimed the Gospel to the household of Cornelius and God poured out His Spirit upon them and they believed in Jesus and were baptized. Few of us can understand the radical nature of this transition to the Jewish mind. For more than two thousand years THEY had seen themselves as the chosen people of God. And, indeed, they were exactly that! Almighty God had chosen Israel, the descendants of Abraham, out of all the nations of the earth to display His wisdom, power and glory. Their very existence as a nation was due to God's direct intervention on their behalf. Apart from Him, they would have most certainly been destroyed, as other nations before them.

Now they were being told that God was broadening His dealings with mankind to include the Gentile nations around them. Their distinction as the people of God seemed threatened, and their identity as a nation was, in their minds, on the verge of being lost. What about God's plans to restore the throne of David? What about God's promise to defeat all the enemies of Israel and to give them the land originally given to Abraham and to have a King who would rule over them who would lead them into an age of peace and righteousness? Were these promises now lost forever? Had their disobedience caused God to forsake them forever?

These are questions which must have been on the minds of some of the Jewish people, even the apostles. And yet, God had commanded them to take the Gospel to ALL people, and they must obey Him. As the number of believers among the Gentiles began to grow and it was obvious that they, too, had received the Spirit of God, missionaries were sent out to areas around Jerusalem, fulfilling Jesus' command to begin in Jerusalem, but to go out from there to the far corners of the world. The first evangelism was done by Jews, and the first Christian missionaries were Jews!

Paul and Barnabas were sent out by the Church to the Gentiles and as they preached they went first to Jews. They went to the synagogue and proclaimed that Jesus was the Messiah, quoting various Old Testament Scriptures to support their claims. But when the Jewish leaders saw the large crowds of people gathered to hear them, they were jealous and they began to speak negatively to the people about these "wandering preachers."

But Paul was not one to back down, so he answered them, saying,

> "We had to speak the Word of God to you first. Since you reject it and do not consider yourselves worthy of eternal life, we now turn to the Gentiles. For this is what the LORD has commanded us: 'I have made you a light for the Gentiles, that you may bring salvation to the ends of the earth'" (Acts 13:46–47).

This became somewhat of a theme for Paul as he wrote his letters to the churches where he was privileged to preach the life-giving message of salvation through faith in Jesus: To the Jew first, then to the Gentiles. We will talk more about that in the next chapter. Among the questions being asked in the early days of the Church was not, "What do we do with Jews who believe?" but rather, "What do we do with Gentiles who believe?"

From the beginning, the concern of those who believed in Jesus was the relationship of the "Christian," as those who believed in Jesus were now being called (Acts 11:26), to the Law of God, not only the Ten Commandments—considered to be the "moral" standard set by God—but also the other laws given in the books of Moses, the "Torah," or the "Book of the Law."

Jesus, in His "Sermon on the Mount," recorded in Matthew 5–7, had already pointed out that He had not come to destroy the law, but rather, to fulfill it. But what about the sacrifices and the feasts of Israel and the other ceremonies which God had given to point ahead to the coming of the Savior and the sacrifice which He would offer to satisfy God's justice and bring forgiveness to those who believed? Were all of these observances fulfilled in Jesus and no longer applicable to those who now accepted Jesus as the promised Messiah?

Today, among the Jews who are coming to faith in Jesus, these same questions are being asked. And it is important for all who study God's Word and who care about obedience to God's revealed will to ask: "What does GOD require of those who believe?" Whatever God requires today should be the same as that which He required in the days of the early Church. God does not have one standard for one period of history and another for a different time; His law and His commands do not change. Psalm 119, as well as other Psalms, speaks admirably about God's law and how important it is for a right understanding of God's will, and reveals the blessing of God upon those who keep it.

So what is it, exactly, that the Jews AND the Gentiles in the early Church were called upon to obey? In order to answer that question, the leaders in Jerusalem called the first church "council" meeting. The specific question which they were being called upon to discuss was this: "Can the Gentiles be saved without receiving the sign of the covenant which God gave to Abraham and his descendants, namely, circumcision?"

Some of the believers who belonged to the party of the Pharisees, religious teachers who had accepted Jesus as the Messiah, argued that the Gentiles must be circumcised and required to obey the Law of Moses. However, after much debate and discussion, led by the Spirit of God these men decided to send a letter to the Gentile churches requiring only that they abstain from eating food that had been sacrificed to idols, from the meat of strangled animals and from sexual immorality (Acts 15:29). Nothing else was said about obedience to the Law as it was enumerated in great detail in Exodus and Leviticus.

From this time on a "division" existed within the Church, as those who were Jewish believers often clung to some of the "traditions" of the temple worship, while others, along with the Gentiles, adopted a much "simpler" worship and life, considering what was called the "ceremonial law" to be fulfilled in Christ and no longer necessary for the Christian to observe.

In his letter to the Colossians, the Apostle Paul spoke to this "debate" with these instructions to the believers:

> "For in Christ all the fullness of the Deity lives
> in bodily form, and you have been given fullness
> in Christ, who is the head over every power and

> authority. In Him you were also circumcised, in the putting off of the sinful nature, not with a circumcision done by the hands of men but with the circumcision done by Christ, having been buried with Him in baptism and raised with Him through the power of God, who raised Him from the dead" (Colossians 2:9–12).

Believing that the Spirit of God "inspired" the writers of the New Testament as He did the writers of the Old Testament, these are God's instructions to the Church for all ages. Circumcision, the sign of God's promises given to Abraham and his descendants until the appearance of the Messiah, the Christ, was now fulfilled in a "spiritual circumcision" of the heart, performed by the very Spirit of God who first commanded Abraham that he and his descendants should be circumcised physically. There are other passages of Scripture which also refer to this change in this new era of God's dealings with mankind. It is not something different, but the fulfillment of what the old pointed towards.

Paul goes on in Colossians to explain these things further:

> "When you were dead in your sins and in the uncircumcision of your sinful nature, God made you alive with Christ. He forgave us all our sins, having cancelled the written code, with its regulations, that was against us and that stood opposed to us; He took it away, nailing it to the cross" (Colossians 2:13–14).

God's Law, as it was revealed through Moses, pointed out mankind's fallen condition and our indebtedness to God. Paul wrote that "through the law we become conscious of sin" (Romans 3:20) and that the law

> ". . . was added because of transgressions until the 'Seed' to who the promise referred had come" (Galatians 3:19).

And further,

> "Before this faith came, we were held prisoners by the law, locked up until faith should be revealed. So the law was put in charge to lead us to Christ that we might be justified by faith. Now that faith has come, we are no longer under the supervision of the law" (Galatians 3:23–24).

This new relationship of Christians, those who accepted Jesus as the promised Messiah, to the law revealed through Moses is further explained in the eighth chapter of Paul's letter to the Romans:

> "Therefore, there is no condemnation to those who are in Christ Jesus, because through Christ Jesus the law of the Spirit of life set me free from the law of sin and death. For what the law was powerless to do in that it was weakened by the sinful nature, God did by sending His own Son in the likeness of sinful man, in order that the righteous requirements of the law might be fully met in us, who do not live according to the sinful nature, but according to the Spirit" (Romans 8:1–4).

Contrary to those who believe that not even the Ten Commandments, let alone any other of the laws God gave Israel, apply to Christians today, God says that the work of His Spirit within us moves us to be "law-keepers" rather than "law-breakers." We are now able to see the wisdom of God's laws and His Spirit gives us the desire to keep them, even as God had promised in Ezekiel 36:26–27. As we saw in the last chapter, the Gospel which the Church proclaimed to the world was that "righteousness" could not be earned through obedience to the Law because no one could keep it. Rather, true righteousness, that which can stand before the judgment seat of Christ, must be received by faith in Jesus. As God credited Abraham's faith to him as righteousness, so He credits the faith of all who believe as righteousness before Him. The perfect righteousness of Jesus becomes ours when we believe in Him as Savior and receive Him as our LORD.

At the same time, the Spirit of God works in the hearts of all true believers and gives to them the desire to be obedient to God's law, to the Ten Commandments and other commands given in God's Word.

As Moses wrote in Deuteronomy 6:5 and as Jesus quoted his words in Matthew 22:37–40, love for God and love for our neighbor is required of every person who claims to know Jesus.

As for the "ceremonial law" and the feast days celebrated by Israel as a nation, as the people of God, we return to Paul's letter to the Colossians and read,

> "Therefore, do not let anyone judge you by what you eat or drink, or with regard to a religious festival, a New Moon celebration or a Sabbath day. These are a shadow of the things that were to come; the reality, however, is found in Christ" (Colossians 2:16–17).

Whether or not the Jewish believers continued to celebrate the feast days and to observe the strict dietary laws and other laws of Exodus and Leviticus is unclear. When the temple was destroyed in 70 a.d., whatever remained of the Old Testament system of worship disappeared along with it. Beyond any doubt, if one accepts the testimony of Scripture, is that God's intention was to bring Jew and Gentile together into one body—the Church. And He accomplished that by fulfilling His promises to the Jews, His covenant with Abraham, and bringing the Gentiles into the people of God through the same faith which Abraham had, which had been credited to him as righteousness before God. We will look into this more closely in the next chapter.

The Gospel was the same for Jew and Gentile, that the righteousness which is needed to stand before God cannot be accomplished through obedience to the Law because no one can keep it perfectly. Rather, God has provided a way through faith in the Messiah to receive HIS righteousness as a gift. Paul, who had as a Pharisee trusted in his own keeping of the law to be good enough to withstand God's judgment, now wrote to the church in Rome,

> "I am not ashamed of the gospel, because it is the power of God for the salvation of everyone who believes: first for the Jew, then for the Gentile. For in the Gospel a righteousness from God is revealed, a righteousness that is by faith from first

to last, just as it is written: 'The righteous will live by faith'" (Romans 1:16–17).

In the sacrifice of Jesus on the cross, God provided the ONLY way for anyone to be saved, Jew or Gentile, for only in the perfect obedience of Jesus was God's justice satisfied. To the Corinthians, Paul wrote,

> "God was reconciling the world to himself in Christ. . . . God made Him who had no sin to BE sin for us, so that in Him WE might become the righteousness of God" (II Corinthians 5:19, 21).

This was and is the Gospel which God called the Church, made up of Jews and Gentiles, to proclaim. As we go on into the next chapter, we will look more closely into God's purpose in establishing the Church, bringing Jews and Gentiles together into one body. God always has a reason for everything He does, and His plan from the beginning was to gather a people who would know Him, love Him and serve Him. No one can thwart God's plan!

The religion of the New Testament, preached by the Apostles, explained and proclaimed by the first Christians, the religion which spread through much of the then-known world even amidst horrible persecution, was NOT a new religion, but the fulfillment of all of God's promises to Abraham, the one whom He had called to be the "father of nations," the one to whom God said, "I will be your God and you will be My people," and your descendants will be as "the stars of the sky and the sand of the seashore."

God had said, "In your 'Seed' ALL nations on the earth will be blessed" (Genesis 12:3). In the resurrection and ascension of Jesus, and the pouring out of the Holy Spirit, those Jews who believed saw the faithfulness of the God of Abraham, Isaac and Jacob and were moved to embrace His Son as their Messiah, their Savior, and to live and die for Him. As the Gospel was carried to the Gentiles, God's plan did not start over, it continued just as He had planned from eternity past.

More and more clearly God revealed His plan and His purpose through His Son Jesus Christ, a plan that has yet to reach its ultimate fulfillment when He returns to earth in order to establish His eternal kingdom. The Church was and is God's idea. Those who believe in Jesus and who, by the power of God's Spirit working in them, desire to please Him and serve Him, are also called to be His witnesses in our world today. Jesus calls believers "the light of the world" and "the salt of the earth" (Matthew 5:13–14).

Much of the Church today has lost its identity, and thus, its sense of "mission." As more and more churches look for a fresh "vision" from God, the need is to return to God's Word and to hear His call to testify to the truth He has revealed there—that Jesus is the Way, the Truth and the Life, and that no one comes to the Father except through Him (John 14:6). Since the Church is God's idea, only those who truly accept Jesus as their Savior and who surrender to Him as their LORD are truly members of God's kingdom. The rest, though they may be perceived as "religious" by those around them, are still dead in sin and in danger of facing God's judgment.

God offers good news, but this Gospel message demands a response that most are not willing to give. God calls all people to repentance, to a change, a turn, a transformation of heart and mind. A few simple, outward religious acts cannot atone for your sin before a holy God. God has not established the Church through the centuries since Jesus walked the earth in order to entertain people or to tell them what they want to hear. Paul writes to the believers in Corinth,

> "For we are to God the aroma of Christ among those who are being saved and those who are perishing. To the one we are the smell of death; to the other, the fragrance of life" (II Corinthians 2:15–16).

God kept His promise to Abraham to provide the sacrifice for sin. And through the Church God now calls people to receive HIS Savior, the Messiah, Jesus. Have you done that? Have you come to see Jesus as the ONLY Mediator who can bring you back to God? Do you understand that only HIS blood can cleanse you of your sin and guilt in God's sight? Will you confess your sin and accept Jesus as your Savior, and then surrender to Him as your LORD and King? God's Spirit works through God's Word to bring about these changes in the hearts and minds of His chosen people, Jews and Gentiles.

You can know that you are one of these people if, by faith, you put your trust in Jesus. The Apostle John writes,

> "Anyone who believes in the Son of God has this testimony in his heart. Anyone who does not believe God has made him out to be a liar, because he has not believed the testimony God has given about his Son. And this is the testimony: God has given us eternal life, and this life is in his Son. He who has the Son has life; he who does not have the Son of God does not have life. I write these things to you who believe in the name of the Son of God so that you may know that you have eternal life" (I John 5:10–13).

When you understand and accept these things, then you can join with others who know Him in making the Church today what GOD wants it to be: a loving, caring body of believers who share their faith and their lives with other people, displaying God's love in word and deed.

It's not enough to just "join" a church; you must be a member of THE Church, the body known only to God, made up of those who have come to know Jesus as the Christ, the Messiah, the promised Savior, the fulfillment of God's promises. May God move your heart to respond to His call today to receive Jesus as YOUR Savior and to join with His people in proclaiming His name until He comes again!

Questions for Reflection:

God had promised Abraham that through his "seed," his descendant, ALL nations on earth would be blessed. This promise was fulfilled as the good news, the Gospel of Jesus Christ, went out into the world, being proclaimed to Jews AND Gentiles. All believers were joined together into one body, the Church of Jesus Christ.

1. Why is it significant that most of the first believers were Jews?

2. Explain how Christianity is Judaism fulfilled.

3. How does the Law of God, first given to the people of Israel, point people to Jesus for forgiveness and life?

4. How does the Spirit of God apply God's Law to the life of those who believe in Jesus? What place does it have in the Church today?

Chapter 11

"Jews and Gentiles: Two Peoples, One Faith"

One religion for all people on earth!? Can it really be?? Is there only one way to have eternal life? If you have searched the Scriptures with us up to this point, you have seen the progressive nature of God's revelation from the beginning of time until today. Our understanding of God's plan, in view of the writings of the prophets and apostles, should be better, clearer than those who lived in the days of the prophets or the days of Jesus or the days of the apostles. Yet, Satan, the deceiver, continues to confuse and deceive. Countless millions will spend eternity facing the judgment of God because they have not heard of Jesus and have not put their faith in Him.

But you are reading this book, and as we look at Scripture after Scripture you are hearing God's voice. To you has been given the privilege to hear and, LORD willing, to understand God's plan. It was to people just like you and me that the Gospel was first preached: to Jews and to Gentiles the same Gospel, the same offer of forgiveness through faith in Jesus.

As we just read, in his letter to the Romans the apostle Paul wrote,

> "I am not ashamed of the Gospel, because it is the power of God for the salvation of everyone who believes; first for the Jew, then for the Gentile" (Romans 1:16).

As he calls his readers to repent, to confess their sin and turn to God for forgiveness and new life by His Spirit, Paul warns them with these words:

> "Because of your stubbornness and your unrepentant heart, you are storing up wrath against yourself for the day of God's wrath, when His righteous judgment will be revealed. God 'will give to each person according to what he has done.' (Psalm 62:12).
>
> To those who by persistence in doing good seek glory, honor and immortality, He will give eternal life. But for those who are self-seeking and who reject the truth and follow evil, there will be wrath and anger. There will be trouble and distress for every human being who does evil; first for the Jew, then for the Gentile; but glory, honor and peace for everyone who does good; first for the Jew, then for the Gentile. For God does not show favoritism" (Romans 2:5–11).

God does not show favoritism! This was a new revelation because up until now He HAD shown favoritism, at least in part. He had chosen a nation of people, completely by grace, and had passed by other nations. The people of Israel had had opportunity after opportunity to know God and to serve Him. But, with few exceptions, they had followed their own way, they had given in to the temptations of Satan and sin, and had rejected God's reign over them.

But we shall see that God's plan to gather a people for Himself was revealed in stages through the centuries in order that we today might understand these things and live to proclaim His kingdom, to be His witnesses to all the nations of the world. God did not change His mind, or go to "Plan B," but carried out His plan to the letter, now bringing Jew AND Gentile together into one body, the Church.

We have seen that Judaism had become a religion mixed with political aspirations for the nation of Israel. Rather than a religion for all people, it had become tied exclusively to the nation of Israel. One of the arguments of the leaders of the Jews for the crucifixion of Jesus was that He was causing a commotion among the people with all of His talk about the kingdom of God, and they were afraid that the Romans would punish the whole nation should Jesus lead a rebellion against the Roman government. It was better, they reasoned, that Jesus should die, than that the whole nation be destroyed.

Now, after the resurrection, as the number of those who believed that Jesus was the promised Messiah increased, the Jews who believed understood that this was the time which the prophets had spoken about, the time when God would fulfill His plan to include the Gentiles as part of His family. The clearest description of this can be found in Paul's letter to the Ephesians.

After explaining the spiritual blessings which come to those who believe in Jesus, both Jews AND Gentiles, Paul speaks specifically to the Gentile believers among them, by far the majority in the congregations founded during Paul's missionary journeys. In the second chapter of Ephesians, Paul writes,

> "Therefore remember that formerly you who are Gentiles by birth and called 'uncircumcised' by those who call themselves 'the circumcision'– remember that at that time you were separate from Christ, excluded from citizenship in Israel and foreigners to the covenants of promise, without hope and without God in the world" (Ephesians 2:11–12).

Up until this time in the history of mankind, God had dealt with Jews and Gentiles differently. To the Jews He had given His written Word, and to Abraham and his descendants God had entered into a covenant relationship in which God had made promises to those who believed. Some of those promises were conditional promises, and when Israel rejected God and worshiped idols, they faced the consequences of their actions. But other promises were unconditional, such as the promise to send a Savior who would rule over Israel at some future time, and the promise that all nations on earth would be blessed through the "Seed" of Abraham, the descendant of Judah, the Son of David.

Gentiles, all those who were NOT Jews, not related to Abraham physically, were outside of the covenant God had made with Israel. While God demonstrated His grace and pointed ahead to this "time of salvation" by including a small number of Gentiles who believed in "Israel's God" during the Old Testament days, the nations of the world played no part in God's plan to gather a people for Himself. Until . . . until Jesus came and the Holy Spirit was poured out and the Gospel of Jesus Christ was brought to them as well as to the Jews.

Now, these two peoples, who had been poles apart spiritually, were being united through faith in Jesus Christ. As the Apostle Paul continued his letter to the church in Ephesus, he explained how Jesus reconciled ALL who believed through His sacrifice on the cross and that through Him peace with God was now being offered to all people through the Gospel. He says, "Through Him we both have access to the Father by one Spirit" (Ephesians 2:18).

In a key text, Paul explains clearly that those Gentiles who accept Jesus as their Savior and LORD are brought into a relationship with God and become equal partners with Jewish believers as part of the chosen people of God.

> "You are no longer foreigners and aliens, but fellow citizens with God's people and members of God's household, built on the foundation of the apostles and prophets, with Christ Jesus Himself as the chief cornerstone. In Him the whole building is joined together and rises to become a holy temple in the LORD. And in Him you too are being built together to become a dwelling in which God lives by His Spirit" (Ephesians 2:19–22).

Going on, Paul explains the progressive nature of God's revelation of His plan to gather a "people" to belong to Him when in chapter 3 he writes,

> "In reading this, then, you will be able to understand my insight into the mystery of Christ, which was not made known to men in other generations as it has now been revealed by the Spirit to God's holy apostles and prophets. This mystery is that through the gospel the Gentiles are heirs together with Israel, members together of one body, and sharers together in the promise in Christ Jesus" (Ephesians 3:4–6).

These things WERE new, but they were new NOT because God had given up on Israel and had decided to go with a different plan to gather a people for Himself. These things were new because God revealed His plan one step at a time, using the nation of Israel to reveal His glory, His holiness and His justice, but also His mercy, His compassion and His grace. Then, in the fullness of time, God had prepared the world for the next step—the coming of the Messiah and the pouring out of His Spirit—both predicted in the Scriptures of the Old Testament; and now God revealed exactly how He was going to fulfill the promise He had given to Abraham that in His Seed all nations on earth would be blessed. God was including the Gentiles as part of His chosen people by faith in the Jewish Messiah!

God had chosen Israel to reveal Himself to the world, and in many ways Israel had fulfilled that purpose. Through His laws and commands God revealed His wisdom and glory; through His protection over Israel and the miraculous deliverance from their slavery in Egypt and from other enemies, God revealed His power and faithfulness. This nation which God had chosen to belong to Him above all the other nations of the world, though stubborn and rebellious, revealed God's compassion and grace in a world filled with false gods who did not exist except in the minds of their followers.

In Israel, God revealed His love, a love so genuine, a love so deep, that God continued to love even after Israel worshiped idols and rejected God as their King. Even though He brought judgment upon them, God's love for Israel, the descendants of Abraham, Isaac and Jacob, never waned. We will see that God has not forgotten Israel or His love for them. They remain His special people as a nation and God is working among the Jewish people today as never before.

But in this time, what the Bible consistently calls the "time of salvation," God is working through the Church to reveal Himself to the world and to accomplish His purposes. Once again, in his letter to the Ephesians, the Apostle Paul explains God's plan in words clear enough for all to understand,

> "Grace was given to me to preach to the Gentiles the unsearchable riches of Christ, and to make plain to everyone the administration of this mystery, which for ages past was kept hidden in God,

who created all things. His intent was that now, through the Church, the manifold wisdom of God should be made known to the rulers and authorities in the heavenly realms, according to His eternal purpose which He accomplished in Christ Jesus our LORD" (Ephesians 3:8–11).

Paul had persecuted Christians, particularly Jewish Christians, because he believed that they were perverting the true religion and rejecting the Word of God. But after he had come face to face with Jesus on the road to Damascus and been filled with the Spirit of God, his mind was opened and he realized that these things were happening as the fulfillment of God's plan from eternity! "According to His eternal purpose," Paul writes! God's purpose was that NOW, through the Church, the manifold wisdom of God should be made known!!

God was not changing His mind; He was not creating a new religion, but rather, He was fulfilling His promises made to Abraham and through Jesus was establishing a new "era," a new "time" when ALL who believed could come to God through faith in Jesus Christ and receive forgiveness and eternal life. Again, we hear Paul's words to the Romans,

"It is with your heart that you believe and are justified (declared innocent), and it is with your mouth that you confess and are saved. As the Scripture says, 'Anyone who trusts in Him will never be put to shame.' For there is no difference between Jew and Gentile–the same LORD is LORD of all and richly blesses all who call on Him, for 'Everyone who calls on the name of the LORD will be saved'" (Romans 10:10–13).

Abraham was saved not by works but by faith! Remember Genesis 15:6: "Abraham believed God and it was credited to him as righteousness." Explaining Abraham's faith in Romans chapter four, Paul writes,

"He (Abraham) is the father of all who believe but have not been circumcised, in order that righteousness might be credited to them. AND he is the father of the circumcised who not only are circumcised but who also walk in the footsteps of the faith that our father Abraham had BEFORE he was circumcised. It was NOT through the law that Abraham and his offspring received the promise that he would be heir of the world, but through the righteousness that comes by faith" (Romans 4:11–13).

Jews and Gentiles are brought together in the Church as they both place their faith in the Messiah, the promised Savior, the "Seed" of Abraham, the descendant of Judah and David. Jews are still Jews and Gentiles are still Gentiles, physically. But spiritually, they are united in ONE body, the Church, the family of God. Paul expresses this unity again in Galatians chapter 3,

"You are all sons of God through faith in Christ Jesus, for all of you who were baptized into Christ have clothed yourselves with Christ. There is neither Jew nor Greek (another word for Gentile), slave nor free, male nor female, for you are all one in Christ Jesus. If you belong to Christ, then you are Abraham's seed, and heirs according to the promise" (Galatians 3:26–29).

Can there be any doubt that the Church was GOD's idea, designed to fulfill His promise to Abraham that in His "Seed" all nations on earth would be blessed? Judaism, with its ties to the Old Testament, is not a "false" religion, but an incomplete one! Jesus and the apostles clearly point out the fulfillment of the Old Testament Scriptures in the birth, life, ministry, death, resurrection and ascension of Jesus, and they point to further fulfillment in the future, again in fulfillment of the Old Testament prophecies concerning Israel and the entire world.

To the Church, Christians, has been given the task to go to the far corners of the world to proclaim the Gospel of Jesus Christ. Jesus Himself spoke often of this task to the disciples, and after His resurrection He gave this commission to them and to all who would come after them:

> "All authority in heaven and on earth has been given to Me. Therefore, go and make disciples of all nations, baptizing them in the name of the Father and of the Son and of the Holy Spirit, and teaching them to obey everything I have commanded you. And surely, I am with you always, to the very end of the age" (Matthew 28:18–20).

And Luke records these words of Jesus shortly before His ascension into heaven:
"This is what is written: The Christ will suffer and rise from the dead on the third day, and repentance and forgiveness of sins will be preached in His name to all nations, beginning at Jerusalem. You are witnesses of these things."

And again, at the beginning of the book of Acts Jesus reveals the mission of the disciples, now apostles sent out into the world, and through them, the mission of all who believe:

> "You will receive power when the Holy Spirit comes upon you; and you will be my witnesses in Jerusalem, and in all Judea and Samaria, and to the ends of the earth" (Acts 1:8).

God not only gave to the apostles and the early Church this "mission" to proclaim the Gospel, but gave them reason to be zealous, to be motivated, explaining that NO ONE could be saved from their sins without believing in Jesus Christ!! Eternal life hung in the balance for all who had never believed in Jesus. "God so loved the world that He gave His only Son, that whoever BELIEVES in Him should have eternal life" (John 3:16). "He who has the Son has life; he who does not have the Son of God does not have life" (I John 5:12).

Today most people believe that all religions are the same, and that Christianity falls into the mix somewhere. Even many within the Church, including many leaders within the Christian community, seek to be "one" with those who do not acknowledge Jesus as "the Christ," the Messiah, the promised Savior. Lack of understanding of the Old

Testament prophecies, of the teaching of Jesus and the apostles concerning the fulfillment of those prophecies in Jesus, and of the biblical mandate to preach this gospel which is the "power of God unto salvation to everyone who BELIEVES" has robbed the Church of the one and only instrument which God has entrusted to the Church to bring about repentance and faith which lead to forgiveness and eternal life.

Christianity cannot be lumped together with all the other religions of the world without losing the very heart of what true biblical Christianity is—the ONE, TRUE religion, established by God to reveal Himself to the world, a world in darkness, without God and without hope! Some people in the United States talk about our "Judaeo-Christian" heritage, referring to the foundations of our faith, but they fail to make the distinction between the "Judaism" of today which rejects Jesus as the Messiah, and the true Judaism of the Bible which looked forward to the coming of the Messiah and which rightly acknowledged Jesus as the Promised One. The "Judaism" of the Pharisees was a man-made religion designed to maintain the identity of the Jewish nation, but which left its followers spiritually dead, much like the religions of the world today.

Jews and Gentiles alike need to rightly understand what the whole Bible says about God and HIS plan of salvation. NONE of this comes from the ideas of mankind. Everything the Bible teaches comes from the very heart and mind and mouth of God, spoken through the writers who were "inspired," led by the very Spirit of God. The Bible does not present two separate, distinct religions; rather, it presents the progressive revelation of God's purpose to reveal Himself and to gather for Himself a people from every nation to belong to Him and to inherit the universe—to experience eternal life with Him, our Creator.

Peter writes,

> "Above all, you must understand that no prophecy of Scripture came about by the prophet's own interpretation. For prophecy never had its origin in the will of man, but men spoke from God as they were carried along by the Holy Spirit" (II Peter 1:21).

As the early Church began to proclaim this message to the world it faced severe persecution. In many places today, those who faithfully proclaim the same message face the same persecution. What keeps them going? What motivates them to endure suffering for the sake of this Gospel? Their conviction that

> "Salvation is found in no one else, for there is no other name under heaven given to men by which we must be saved" (Acts 4:12).

People without Jesus are lost and in danger of facing God's eternal judgment. Nations and peoples are being deceived, and many even within the Church today are being deceived into believing that believing in some generic "God" and being "religious" will get you to heaven some day. Denominations and church leaders refuse to proclaim that Jesus is "the Way, the Truth and the Life," and that "NO ONE comes to the Father, except through Him" (John 14:6). Instead, they twist and distort the Word of God to allow for God's grace to reach even those who do not know Him.

In reality, these prove that they do not know GOD! All of mankind exists before a holy God and deserves His just judgment. There is no such thing as an "innocent" child or adult. Mankind has rejected God since the Garden of Eden and faces the just judgment of a holy God. The ONLY hope is found in God's provision of the perfect sacrifice for sin: His own Son, Jesus Christ, the "Lamb of God who takes away the sin of the world" (John 1:29). In His Name, forgiveness has been offered, and continues to be offered, through all the world.

Sometimes people forget that the Gospel began to be preached in Jerusalem. The early Church existed in the Middle East and spread from there to Asia and Africa and Europe. All these peoples, all these nations, have had the opportunity to know God. In Europe today cathedrals stand nearly empty as monuments to the failure of those who heard the Gospel to teach their children and grandchildren. The same is happening today in the United States of America.

Unless we begin to take seriously the great commission, unless we begin to study God's Word and to understand the truth of the Gospel message, that only by believing in Jesus, by accepting Him as the Messiah, confessing our sins and asking God's forgiveness, can any person receive eternal life, the souls of millions will be on our heads. In Ezekiel 33, the LORD told Ezekiel that he was a "Watchman," and that to him was given the responsibility to warn others that judgment was coming and to offer them salvation. He says,

> "If the watchman sees the sword coming and does not blow the trumpet to warn the people and the sword comes and takes the life of one of them, that man will be taken away because of his sin, but I will hold the watchman accountable for his blood" (Ezekiel 33:6).

With Jude, the writer of a brief letter which lies just before the book of Revelation in the Bible, I write to my brothers and sisters in the Church today,

> "Dear friends, although I was very eager to write to you about the salvation we share, I felt I had to write and urge you to contend for the faith that was once for all entrusted to the saints" (Jude 3).

"The faith!" There is only ONE true faith, only one true Gospel, only one true religion that leads to eternal life. There is only ONE body of believers, made up of Jews and Gentiles who have accepted the testimony of God through His Word and Spirit, who believe that Jesus is the Christ, the Son of the living God. Jesus promised that He would build His Church upon THIS "rock." In the fourth chapter of Ephesians, Paul encouraged those who knew Christ Jesus as Savior and LORD with these words,

> "Make every effort to keep the unity of the Spirit through the bond of peace. There is one body and one Spirit–just as you were called to one hope when you were called–one LORD, one faith, one baptism; one God and Father of all, who is over all and through all and in all" (Ephesians 4:3–6).

Then, going on to explain how God has chosen to work in the Church and through the Church, He says of Christ,

> "It was He who gave some to be apostles, some to be prophets, some to be evangelists, and some to

be pastors and teachers, to prepare God's people for works of service, so that the body of Christ may be built up until we all reach unity in the faith and in the knowledge of the Son of God" (Ephesians 4:11–13).

Truth exists today, as it has since the beginning; truth revealed from God to human beings, to mankind, to people just like you and me. Whether or not people accept the truth does not change the truth, but whether or not people accept God's truth determines whether they have eternal life or will face eternal death.

God's Word continues to be proclaimed today, to Jews and to Gentiles, calling all people to faith in the Savior God Himself has provided, Jesus Christ, the Messiah. Through faith in Him the lost are being found and spirits that were enslaved by ignorance and sin are being set free. May God use even the words written on these pages to call some out of darkness, to behold His marvelous light, to come to Him through faith in Jesus Christ and receive the gift of eternal life!!

Questions for Reflection:

Christianity is either the only true religion, or it is a false religion, because Jesus claims to be the only way to be reconciled to God, our Creator. Those who believe in Jesus are ambassadors for Christ, proclaiming the truth which God has revealed by His Word and Spirit.

1. In the church there is no distinction between Jews and Gentiles. What is the basis for our unity?

2. What is this time period in God's plan called? Why?

3. What task or mission has God given to the Church today?

4. To whom is the Church called to proclaim the one and only true Gospel message?

Chapter 12:

"Has the Church Replaced Israel?"

"Yes, and No." Though most within the Church today see no place for the Jews and Israel in God's plans, the truth is that the question, "Has the Church replaced Israel?" is an incomplete question, and any time you ask an incomplete question you get, at best, an incomplete, if not completely incorrect answer. First, we need to ask the right questions and then we need to allow GOD to give us the answer, rather than trying to come up with our own.

Clearly, Israel as a nation faced the judgment of God centuries before Jesus was born. Having rejected God as their King, they were driven from their land and the nation of Israel ceased to exist, at least to the human eye. A small part of the descendants of Abraham, the nation of Judah, having suffered through seventy years of exile and captivity in Babylon, returned to the land in fulfillment of God's Word, rebuilt the temple, and remained a nation, albeit one under foreign rulers, until the birth of Jesus. This was necessary to fulfill God's promise that the Savior, the coming King, would descend from Judah, one of Jacob's sons, and that He would be born in Bethlehem.

Shortly after Jesus ascended into heaven the nation of Judah was destroyed, along with the temple in Jerusalem. From this time on, until 1948, the physical descendants of Abraham did not exist as a nation in the land which God had promised to Abraham and his descendants, though the Jews continued to exist as a distinct people in various places throughout the world.

Understandably, many believed that all of God's promises to Israel as a nation were "transferred" to the Church and that the Church became a type of "spiritual Israel." However, since the nation of Israel was re-established in the same land God gave to Abraham and since hundreds of thousands of Jews have returned to the land over the past few decades, more and more people are beginning to see that God takes His promises seriously, and that a literal understanding of God's Word leads to a clearer understanding of what is happening in our world today and what lies ahead in the future.

When the prophet Jeremiah spoke of a "new covenant" which God would make with Israel in future days, he said that there would be a time when all of the "house of Israel" would know the LORD and receive His forgiveness. In Jeremiah 31, verses 35–36, God commits Himself to Israel when He says,

> "This is what the LORD says, He who appoints the sun to shine by day, who decrees the moon and stars to shine by night, who stirs up the sea so that its waves roar–the LORD Almighty is His name: 'Only if these decrees vanish from my sight will the descendants of Israel ever cease to be a nation before Me.'"

In the heart and mind of God the nation of Israel has never ceased to exist. At the end of his book, the prophet Isaiah wrote these words of God,

> "Can a country be born in a day or a nation be brought forth in a moment? Yet no sooner is Zion in labor than she gives birth to her children" (Isaiah 66:8).

So it happened in May, 1948. No other people have ever been exiled from their homeland and re-established as a nation in the same land. This has never happened! Why Israel?? Because God said it would be so!! But does this answer our question?

Let's expand our question in such a way that we can give God's answer and show again that what the Bible says is truth, proving that the Gospel of Jesus Christ is the ONLY way to eternal life. Let's ask our question this way: "Has the Church replaced Israel in God's plan to spread the knowledge of God to the world today?"

The answer to that question is "Yes." Since the birth of the early Church the nation of Israel has not been God's primary instrument to reveal Himself and to invite those who do not believe to come to Him to be saved. That task, that responsibility, that "mission" has been given to the Church of Jesus Christ, a Church made up of Jews and Gentiles, people from every tribe, nation, language and tongue, just as God predicted through the prophets hundreds of years ago.

We have already looked at Ephesians 3, where Paul speaks of the "mystery" which was previously not known, but which God has now made known: "that through the gospel the Gentiles are heirs together with Israel, members together of one body, and sharers together in the promise in Christ Jesus" (Ephesians 3:6). God turned from Israel as His instrument to make Himself known to the Church. In verse ten of this same chapter, Paul says that God's intent "was that NOW, through the Church, the manifold wisdom of God should be made known." The responsibility for revealing God's wisdom and glory and for proclaiming the message of salvation was now laid on the Church. In this way, the Church has, during this "time of salvation" (II Corinthians 6:2), "replaced" Israel.

And like Israel, the Church has been unfaithful in many ways. During the centuries after the early Church began to proclaim the Gospel, the Church turned away from the Word of God and accepted the word of men, establishing traditions much like the religious leaders of the Jews had done before them. The "organized church" during these centuries sought to force people to accept the Gospel by any means and horrible things were done in the name of Christ, things which many have still not forgotten though these things took place centuries ago. For more than a thousand years "Christianity," the only true religion, and the Gospel which the Church was called to proclaim, were perverted and twisted to give political power to kings and rulers and to give to the religious leaders spiritual power over the masses. Such perversion of the true, biblical religion still exists in many places around the world. In fact, many identify Christianity with a religious organization rather than with the Gospel of Jesus Christ and those who truly know and love and desire to serve Him.

Finally, the Church became so corrupt that a movement began which eventually divided the Church and sought to "reform" it. The Reformation, as it was called, re-established the Word of God as the only source of truth and faith in Jesus Christ as the only way to have eternal life. Since that time the world has associated Christianity with the "Dark Ages," when salvation could be "bought" and tyrants often had the blessing of the "Church."

Yet through all this, the TRUE Church, those who accepted Jesus Christ as the promised Messiah, has continued to proclaim the Gospel of Jesus Christ. At the beginning of the Reformation and during this dark period, many true believers gave their lives at the hands of the "church." Those who sought to proclaim the truth that we are saved by grace through faith, and who refused to accept the words of any man above the Word of God, were persecuted and often put to death. In some places around the world this antagonism toward those who preach the real Gospel continues. Many who claim to be "Christian" today do not understand the importance of knowing that faith in Jesus is the ONLY way to have eternal life. Instead, they mix the truth with lies and distortions which leave people confused and frustrated. We have seen that those who believe in Jesus are brought into the covenant relationship which God made with Abraham by faith. While there are many "churches" to choose from in most places today, only those who receive the Bible as the Word of God and who trust completely in Jesus for forgiveness and eternal life are "children of God."

What many see today as "Christianity" may be much like the Judaism which prevailed at the time of Jesus' birth. In the United States religion has become big business. And while there are some who truly know the God who has revealed Himself in the Bible through His Son Jesus Christ, who are filled with the Spirit of God and who desire to worship and serve Him, there are many others who pretend, who are being deceived into believing that merely giving lip service to God is all it takes to get into heaven.

The only true religion is NOT the picture of Christianity that many people have; rather, it is the true work of God in the hearts and minds of people by His Spirit which transforms them from the inside out and makes them followers of the Christ, the Jewish Messiah, Jesus. These people, Jews and Gentiles, make up the true Church. God knows who they are and He is not fooled by the religious ramblings of others who want the glory for themselves.

The destiny of the true Church, of those who truly know and trust Jesus Christ and who acknowledge Him as LORD, accepting His rule over their lives—the destiny of the true Church is clearly revealed in God's Word. Those who die before the return of Jesus Christ go immediately to be with Him in heaven. Their spirits reside with Jesus, awaiting the resurrection of their bodies when He returns. And those who are alive when Jesus returns will be transformed and united with those who have gone before them, to live with Christ forever in His eternal kingdom.

The Apostle Paul writes of this in his first letter to the Christians in Thessalonica, I Thessalonians 4:15–17:

> "According to the LORD's own word, we tell you that we who are alive, who are left till the coming of the LORD, will certainly not precede those who have fallen asleep. For the LORD Himself will come down from heaven, with a loud command, with the voice of the archangel and with the trumpet call of God, and the dead in Christ will rise first. After that, we who are still alive and are left will be caught up together with them in the clouds to meet the LORD in the air. And so we will be with the LORD forever!"

Jesus told His disciples that they would face suffering and tribulation in this life, but that they should not be afraid, for He would be with them. He says the same thing to His disciples today. We are never alone!! God predicts times of suffering, and in fact, He predicts suffering specifically for those in Jerusalem at the end of the age. The Church has been called and gifted by God to proclaim the Gospel to the far corners of the world, just as it is being done today. But this "time of salvation" will come to an end. At that time, God will deal specifically once again with Israel as a nation.

We are living today in what the Bible describes as the "time of salvation." Others have labeled it, "The Church Age," emphasizing the fact that the Church is, today, God's chosen instrument to proclaim His name to the nations. But the Church has NOT replaced Israel in the heart and mind of God. While Jew and Gentile are united together in the Church, God continues to have a plan for Israel AS A NATION, which He does not have for any other nation on the face of the earth. We have seen that "at the present time there is a remnant chosen by grace" (Romans 11:5). Through the Messianic movement God continues to call Jews to believe in Jesus as the Christ, the fulfillment of God's promises to send the Anointed One, the Messiah. Paul goes on to say,

> "What Israel sought so earnestly it did not obtain, but the elect did. The others were hardened. . . . Israel has experienced a hardening *in part* until the full number of the Gentiles has come in. . . . As far as the gospel is concerned, they are (at this time) enemies on your account; but as far as election is concerned, they are loved on account of the patriarchs, for God's gifts and his call are irrevocable" (Romans 11:7,25,28–29).

God continues to call a remnant of the Jews to faith in Jesus even today. The Church must recognize this truth and proclaim the Gospel to Jews as well as to Gentiles. ALL need to hear the Gospel, whether Jew or Gentile. That was true in the first century and it is true today. God has no "special covenant" with Jewish people which excuses them from acknowledging Jesus as the Christ or allows them to enter God's presence in any other way than through His blood. The Gospel was taken "first to the Jews, and then to the Gentiles." Only by hearing the good news of forgiveness and life in Jesus and by embracing Jesus as Savior can anyone be saved from God's wrath.

But, as far as election goes, so far as God's sovereign choice is concerned, Israel as a nation is STILL a special people to God because of His promises to Abraham, Isaac and Jacob. God will make Himself glorious once again as He deals with Israel and comes to her aid in these last days! Though they do not, at this time, accept Jesus as their Messiah, they WILL, according to Zechariah 12. As He speaks through the prophet Zechariah, God says,

> "I will pour out on the house of David and the inhabitants of Jerusalem a spirit of grace and supplication. They will look on me, the one they have pierced, and they will mourn for him as one mourns for an only child, and grieve bitterly for him as one grieves for a firstborn son" (Zechariah 12:10).

There WILL come a time when the Jews, as a nation, will receive Jesus as their Messiah and bow the knee to Him as their LORD. But this will not happen until the nation goes through the time of tribulation which the Bible predicts is coming at the end of THIS age, the Church Age. Jesus speaks clearly about these things in the Gospels and we will look at this at another time. The important thing to understand here is that the Bible tells us that Israel and the Jewish people continue to have a future in God's plans for this world. Why is that important? Because God's truthfulness and faithfulness depend upon this being true!!

Those who would transfer all of the promises God made to Israel over to the Church fail to understand what they are giving up and also place the Church in an extremely dangerous position. God's Word contains very specific promises concerning Israel and Jerusalem. Perhaps we can understand those who have gone before us seeking to apply these things in the only way they thought they could because Israel, as a nation, did not exist for nearly 1900 years. However, as we have seen the progressive nature of God's revelation, we today live in another time of fulfillment. Israel, as a nation, DOES exist today—miraculously so!! And events around us are pointing ever more clearly to the circumstances which will lead the world to the NEXT age.

Jesus promised His disciples and all who would believe in Him through the testimony they would give that He would be with them to the "end of the AGE" (Matthew 28:20). Whatever believers need in order to endure and to continue to trust in Jesus and to be His witnesses, we will receive. Our LORD will not leave us alone; He will not forsake us. God's promises MUST come to pass; for if God can be shown to be a liar at any point, then we have lost our hope and we are, like the rest of mankind, lost in a maze of doubt and fear. God's truthfulness and faithfulness depend upon His keeping His promises made to Abraham, Isaac and Jacob, and through the prophets to Israel and the Jews.

Further, if the sinful disobedience and unfaithfulness of Israel caused God to forsake them, to abandon them, to forget them—then the Church today must know that the same fate awaits us; for who can say that we have not done the same?! If God's promises to Israel were conditional, then God's promises to the Church must also be conditional, and then God's plan must yet have another direction to go, for in many ways the "Church," the organized body with which most identify "Christianity," has strayed and has served other gods as much as Israel ever did.

But the Bible is clear that God's promises to Israel as a nation WILL be kept!

Yes, many thought that the prophecies relating to God's dealing with Israel as a nation must be interpreted symbolically or allegorically because there was no nation of Israel for more than 1900 years! But the re-emergence of Israel as a nation in the land which God gave to Abraham more than four thousand years ago makes it clear that God intends to keep His promises to Israel literally. And the reason for that is obvious: for His glory!!

In Luke 21 Jesus predicted that Jerusalem would be destroyed, along with the temple, and that the Jews would be taken to all the nations. He said that "Jerusalem will be trampled on by the Gentiles until the times of the Gentiles are fulfilled" (Luke 21:24). While God does not make a distinction between Jew and Gentile within the body of the Church, He DOES make a distinction between Israel and the Gentile nations. This is where many people miss God's purpose and the plan which He reveals in Scripture.

Almighty God CHOSE Israel to be a special people to Him. And at some future time, perhaps very soon as we watch the events in the Middle East unfolding before our eyes, God will fight for Israel and defend her against the nations of the world. Israel exists today as a nation for the glory of God. Even though the Jews as a whole have not accepted Jesus as their Messiah, as a nation they hold a special place in God's plan for bringing glory to Himself through them. Once again, in the eleventh chapter of Romans Paul quotes Jeremiah when he predicts a time when God will heal the spiritual blindness of the descendants of Abraham.

> "The deliverer will come from Zion; He will turn godlessness away from Jacob. And this is my covenant with them when I take away their sins" (Romans 11:26–27).

When will this happen? The prophet Zechariah spells out the future events surrounding Israel and Jerusalem in chapters 12–14, as we have already seen in Zechariah 12. We are seeing these things come to pass in our day.

> "I am going to make Jerusalem a cup that sends

> all the surrounding peoples reeling. Judah will be besieged as well as Jerusalem. On that day, when all the nations of the earth are gathered against her, I will make Jerusalem an immovable rock for all the nations" (Zechariah 12:2–3).

In the remainder of chapter 12, Zechariah reveals that God will fight for Israel and defend her against the nations, just as He did in the days of the Kings. But this will be different because the people of Israel will receive the Spirit of God and they will see Jesus, "the one whom they have pierced" (Zechariah 12:10), and they will weep and confess their sin and accept Jesus as their King.

Before Jesus returns, Israel and Jerusalem will face horrible trials and suffering. But at last, just as He promised, Jesus will return and stand on the Mount of Olives and defend Jerusalem, destroying the nations who attack her as He did her enemies in the days of Joshua and David.

Though the Church has in some sense taken the role which Israel had in glorifying God and proclaiming His name to the world, the Church has not been substituted for Israel in God's heart. In future days, God will establish His throne in Jerusalem and Jesus will rule for a thousand years on the earth. Those who have believed in Jesus, Jews and Gentiles, will reign with Jesus in Jerusalem. We will be there, testifying to His love, to His grace, to His wisdom, holiness, justice and power!!

Why have so many today "missed" God's plan for Israel? There are many answers for that question, but the most obvious is that they have not rightly understood and interpreted God's Word. Perhaps we could excuse those who lived before 1948 for seeking to understand the prophecies relating to Israel as a nation when there was no such nation on the earth; but for the past fifty years and more we have been able to see with our own eyes the plan of God unfolding, just as He said it would!

The physical descendants of Abraham have been returning to Israel by the hundreds of thousands while the nations around them have sought to destroy them. The Spirit of God is drawing them to the exact place where God said they would be when Jesus returned to earth. In Romans 11 Paul warns Gentile believers not to become proud, thinking that they are now more important in God's plan than Israel, thinking that the Church has replaced Israel. He writes,

> "Do not boast over those branches. If you do, consider this: You do not support the root, but the root supports you! . . . Do not be arrogant, but be afraid. For if God did not spare the natural branches, he will not spare you either" (Romans 11:18,20–21).

We Gentiles who have believed in Jesus Christ have been "grafted in" to the "natural branches"; and if God brought judgment upon them when they disobeyed and turned away from Him, He will do the same if we act as they did. They became proud of their "status" as the "people of God," and today it seems that many in the Church are doing the same thing. We stand by GRACE—"undeserved favor," nothing else. We have done nothing to earn God's forgiveness or His blessing. On the contrary, like Israel we have been unfaithful to God in so many ways. We, too, have worshiped idols, putting other things before our devotion to God. If Israel was rejected because of their sin, how much more will the Church be rejected for its disobedience to the same God?!

In his Revelation, the Apostle John speaks of the judgment that is soon to come upon the whole earth. We will speak more about that in another book. But this judgment will fall upon all those who do not worship the one true God and who do not come to Him in the only way that HE has described in His Word: through faith in His Son Jesus Christ. There is ONE true religion; there is ONE true faith; there is ONE way to have eternal life.

Do you want to live forever?? Do you want eternal life? Jesus says, "I am the Way, the Truth and the Life; no one comes to the Father except through Me" (John 14:6). The time to come to Jesus, the Christ, the Jewish Messiah, is NOW! This is the "time of salvation." As God Himself closed the door of the ark in the days of Noah before He sent the flood, so He will gather believers out of this world before He pours out His wrath on the earth and all who have not known Him.

All the religions of the world leave mankind in their guilt; none offer any hope of forgiveness from a holy and just God. But the true God SO LOVED the world that He gave His own Son, that whoever believes in Him should have everlasting life (John 3:16). This is your chance; this is your opportunity to make your eternal destination sure. You must confess your sins and be truly sorry for offending the God who created you. You must, in your heart of hearts, desire to turn away from sin and live to please God, in obedience to His commandments. And you must accept Jesus Christ not only as your Savior, as your Mediator, but also as your LORD. You must surrender your life to Him and live no longer for yourself but for Him who gave His all for you. Nothing less will do; but nothing more is needed.

From the beginning of the Bible to the end God has revealed Himself through His Word. He has now revealed Himself to you. He wants you to know Him, to love Him and to serve Him. He wants to have communion with you every moment of every day. As he wrote about the coming time of judgment, the Apostle Peter warns those who do not take God's Word seriously and who think all of this talk about the end of the age and judgment to be foolishness:

> "But do not forget this one thing, dear friends: With the LORD a day is like a thousand years, and a thousand years like a day. The LORD is not slow in keeping His promise, as some understand slowness. He is patient with you, not wanting anyone to perish, but everyone to come to repentance" (II Peter 3:8–9).

Yes, God is being patient with mankind. He continues to offer forgiveness and life in the name of Jesus, though the majority of mankind has rejected His message and refused His invitation for over two thousand years. But Peter goes on,

> "The day of the LORD WILL come like a thief. The heavens will disappear with a roar; the elements will be destroyed by fire, and the earth and everything in it will be laid bare" (II Peter 3:10).

Why do people choose spiritual death when God offers spiritual life and, finally, eternal life in a new heavens and a new earth?? Because they have been deceived by their own sinful nature and by Satan, the devil, the fallen angel who wanted to be God, just as Adam and Eve were deceived in the Garden of Eden. Not much has changed since the beginning of time. But things are about to change!! And only those who know Jesus Christ have a sure and certain hope based on the promises of a faithful God who keeps His covenants.

In the eighth chapter of his letter to the Christians in Rome, the Apostle Paul writes about the privilege of knowing Jesus and being a child of God. He says,

> "Those who are led by the Spirit of God are sons of God. For you did not receive a spirit that makes you a slave again to fear, but you received the Spirit of sonship. And by Him we cry, 'Abba, Father.' The Spirit Himself testifies with our spirit that we are God's children. Now if we are children, then we are heirs–heirs of God and co-heirs with Christ, if indeed we share in His sufferings in order that we may also share in His glory" (Romans 8:14–17).

God does not promise that we who know Him will not face trials and suffering in this life, but He DOES promise that He will be with us, that He will strengthen us, that He will use us to glorify Himself through our testimony and that when we "walk through the valley of the shadow of death" we will not walk alone, but will be led by His hand into His glorious presence. He is the loving Father of those who come to Him through His Son Jesus Christ; and He is forever faithful to those who call upon Him.

Christianity, true biblical Christianity, is the WAY to eternal life in the presence of God—the ONLY WAY!! Based upon God's promises to Abraham, Isaac and Jacob, fulfilled in the coming of the Jewish Messiah, Jesus, and applied to the hearts and minds of those whom God chooses by His Holy Spirit—this one true FAITH will be proclaimed until Jesus Himself stands again upon this earth. May God open your ears to hear His voice; may He open your mind to understand His words, and may He open your heart to receive His Son—for "he who has the Son has life!" (I John 5:12).

Questions for Reflection:

God has had a plan from the beginning and He has kept His promises to send a Savior, the Messiah, and to bless all nations through Jesus, the Christ. And God still has a plan, both for the Church and for the Jews, the descendants of Abraham, as a nation. As He has kept His promises in the past, He WILL keep His promises in the future!!

1. In what way has the Church taken the place of Israel in God's plan for today?

2. What promises has God made concerning Israel, the Jewish nation, for the future?

3. What is the ONLY way for any person to be saved from God's wrath and judgment against sin and to receive the gift of eternal life?

4. What sure and certain hope do those have who believe in Jesus and who thereby receive God's grace TODAY?

Contact Steven Demers
or order more copies of this book at

TATE PUBLISHING, LLC

127 East Trade Center Terrace
Mustang, Oklahoma 73064

(888) 361 - 9473

Tate Publishing, LLC

www.tatepublishing.com